The Balearic Islands

Hazel Thurston

The Balearic Islands
Majorca, Minorca, Ibiza and Formentera

B. T. Batsford Ltd   *London*

First published 1977
© Hazel Thurston 1977
ISBN 0 7134 0882 0

Phototypeset by Trident Graphics Ltd, Reigate, Surrey
Made and printed in Great Britain by
J. W. Arrowsmith Ltd, Bristol
for the publishers
B. T. Batsford Ltd
4 Fitzhardinge Street, London W1H 0AH

Contents

BALEARIC ISLANDS

0   10   50 miles
10   80 km

MAJORCA

S

I. Dragonera

Palma

Andraitx

C. de Cala Figuera

Bahia de Pa

MEDITERRANEAN SEA

Portinatx
S. Juan Bautista
S. Miguel
I. Conejara
San Antonio
Sta. Eulalia del Rio
Ibiza
IBIZA
San José
I. Vedra
I. Espalmador
Cala Sabina
San Francisco Javier
Formentera
C. Berberia

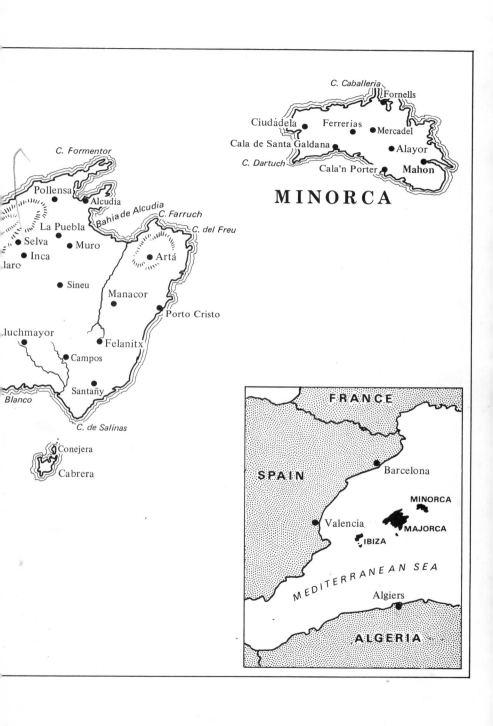

C. Formentor

Pollensa
Alcudia
La Puebla
Bahia de Alcudia
C. Farruch
Selva
C. del Freu
Muro
Inca
laro
Artá
Sineu
Manacor
Porto Cristo
Juchmayor
Felanitx
Campos
Santañy
Blanco
C. de Salinas
Conejera
Cabrera

C. Caballeria
Fornells
Ciudádela
Ferrerias
Mercadel
Cala de Santa Galdana
Alayor
C. Dartuch
Cala'n Porter
Mahon

MINORCA

FRANCE

SPAIN
Barcelona

MINORCA

Valencia
MAJORCA
IBIZA

MEDITERRANEAN SEA

Algiers

ALGERIA

List of Illustrations

Illustrations appear between pages 64–81

The Four Islands

Three principal islands and several smaller ones in one Mediterranean archipelago might reasonably be assumed to be somewhat alike; but this is not true of the Balearics. Nor do they bear close resemblance to mainland Spain, of which together they form a province. Majorca, Minorca and Ibiza each has a character of its own, a sturdy sense of independence, and even slightly dissimilar tongues and exceptional words spoken in the home and market place—though of course Spanish is in general use as the common official language, and out of courtesy to visitors. Because of the many differences between the islands, which even apply to climate, and to some degree to historical trends, they currently attract widely differing types of tourists and expatriate residents. Most generalisations are subject to a margin of error, but it may safely be claimed that Majorca is the Mecca of mass tourism boosted by the authorities and the package tour operators, who have, incidentally, extended their season in the form of long-stay winter holidays which come as a boon and a blessing to retired and sun-starved northerners; that Minorca, with its shorter season and resolute preservation of a dignified mode of life, conditioned by agriculture and local industry, is still being 'discovered' by people who prefer to seek out their own entertainment in relatively peaceful and uncongested surroundings; while Ibiza, in process of casting off a recent reputation for the more unacceptable non-activity of international hippies, still preserves something of the almost South Seas enchantment of a remote island where Man comes close to Nature, time stands still, and everyone 'can do their own thing'.

These are the obvious differences, yet at the moment of writing it is irresistible to turn Devil's Advocate in making the point that Majorca's tourist industry tends to be concentrated along narrow coastal strips, so that its central plain and less accessible shores, with their small towns and harbours, possess a quiet fascination, making for rewarding exploration, while the mountains of the north-west have for many years been the haunt of writers and artists who have discovered there the seclusion which their work and inclinations demand. Minorca has its developments centred on inlets which have been unobtrusively equipped with good hotels, well planned holiday villas and sports facilities, all of which make maximum use of sun, sea and local colour set against a background of cliff scenery and unique archaeological remains. And Ibiza, for all its rural, uninhibited delights, provides well-defined areas which have been committed to catering for entertainments, festivities and the other pleasures of holidaymakers who have a limited time at their disposal and accordingly wish to plunge headlong into all those activities which are associated with the sunny Mediterranean. Each island, in fact, contains a profusion of ingredients which not only blend together, but which may each be isolated and savoured separately.

In remote ages, what is now a group of islands formed part of the mountain range which still extends across mainland Andalusia from near Cadiz on the Atlantic coast of Spain to the Cabo de la Nao, north-east of Alicante on the Costa Blanca. These mountains, folded by geophysical pressures, continue as sub-marine shelves on the Mediterranean seabed, to reappear first as Ibiza and its companion island of Formentera before rearing steeply into peaks as the skeletal north-western back-bone of Majorca. Minorca is further out to sea, with a different and older geological history. This island consists of a cliff-bound plateau with one central eminence, little more than a hill, but from which the whole island and a vast stretch of the Mediterranean is visible. The three Balearics, including their rocky outcrops such as Cabrera off the south coast of Majorca, may be identified romantically as the summits of some lost Atlantis, in the same way as the Islands of Scilly and their watery environment are believed by many people to be remains of England's original south-westerly limits, and one of the sources of Arthurian legend.

In physical terms, the Balearic islands lie from 50-190 miles (80-300 km) off the east coast of Spain. Palma de Mallorca, capital of its own island and also of the province, is the headquarters of the military, judicial and ecclesiastical systems as centralised on the mainland. This city, with its excellent harbour and airport, is 132 miles from Barcelona, 140 from Valencia, 172 from Algiers and 287 from Marseilles. Such a coincidence of neighbours explains many things, including the wide variety of vegetation, such as pines and palms, oranges and almonds, olives and grapes from two continents, as well as the distinct racial types which may be read into the physiognomy of the islanders. The total land area of the archipelago is 1,936 square miles or 5,014 square kilometres.

Not unnaturally, geography has largely dictated the history of the islands. Their position, midway between two continents and not far from the outlet of the Mediterranean to the Atlantic through the Straits of Gibraltar, predestined them to become much coveted and violently contested staging points for military and commercial operations. They were accessible from all quarters as well as being close to the end of lengthy voyages from Tyre and Sidon and other Phoenician ports, Carthage, Rome, Byzantium and, later, the mercantile city states of Italy. When these island harbours and settlements with their docks and warehouses came to be threatened it followed that strongholds had to be built to withstand marauders. Even so, throughout a long history, the coastal settlements remained vulnerable to surprise by pirates, in the same way as peaceable shipping was prey to privateers, which explains why, notably on Majorca, the oldest towns are situated some distance inland from the ports which service them, thus affording their citizens sufficient time for retrenchment and preparation for attack from the moment that danger was heralded. This was done by means of a primitive, but highly effective early warning system, incorporated in the coastal castles and lookout towers, each within signalling distance of a neighbour, which ringed the islands. Such separation of towns into two distinct entities, some distance apart, occurs frequently in Majorca, and the city of Palma is the only one to have been built around its port. Andraitx has for its outpost Puerto de Andraitx, Pollensa –Puerto de Pollensa, Soller Puerto de Soller, and there are several other examples of this defensive way of life made necessary by the circumstances of history, the power politics of the Mediterranean and the continual waves of invasion and conquest by ascendant races.

Each of the three principal islands possesses prehistoric remains in the form of mysterious stone monuments which give little clue to the people who erected them; but documented history may be taken as dating from at least the eleventh century BC, when the Balearics were known to Greek sailors as a landfall near the western limits of the Mediterranean. According to Strabo, the Greek geographer and historian born in 64 or 63 BC, the first settlers came from Rhodes, but it is also known that the Phocaeans, originating from an Ionian city in Asia Minor, had already made a practice of calling at the islands. They colonised Massilia (Marseilles) to the north and Emporion (now Ampurias), once an island stronghold but now joined to the mainland on a stretch of the Costa Brava. The Phocaeans continued to use the Balearics as staging posts well into the sixth century BC But whatever use was made of the islands by foreigners, the natives never allowed themselves to be assimilated into an alien culture.

The Greeks knew Majorca and Minorca as the *Gymnesia,* because of their belief that the natives went naked in summer. Ibiza and Formentera were called the *Pityussae* or Pine islands. Initially the island peoples dwelt in caves, the majority of which were natural hollows and labyrinths in the rocks of cliff or mountain, though in more advanced periods these dwellings were enlarged to form two different types of habitation: one circular with a domed roof, and the other—chiefly used for funerary purposes—a long room with side chambers. A study of these remains, such as have survived at San Vicente, near the north-western corner of Majorca, has led the Institute of Catalan Studies to the conclusion that the islands were inhabited as early as 2000 BC, at the beginning of the Bronze Age.

History becomes clearer with the arrival on the scene of the Carthaginians, who displaced the Phocaeans about 520 BC. This great trading nation, an offshoot of the maritime Phoenicians who were destroyed by the Persian Empire, held the Balearics and Corsica as their chief overseas dominions, and were ruled from Carthage, that incomparable city on the outskirts of Tunis. The capital of Minorca, Mahon, is named after Magon, a Carthaginian general. But powerful though the Punic civilisation was, it in turn fell to the overwhelming imperial might of Rome, culminating in the utter destruction of the mother city in 146 BC at the end of the third and last Punic War. In the previous war of that name, between 218 and 210 BC, the Carthaginians had recruited Majorcan slingers as mercenaries. They participated in the famous offensive against Rome which took them with Hannibal across the Pyrenees and the Alps deep into Italy. These Majorcan warriors were famous in their day. According to the historian Diodorus Siculus, the Sicilian-born author of a 'Universal History' comprising 40 books in three parts, who lived in the 1st century BC, they each were armed with three slings: one held ready for use, the second tied around the head and the third around the belly. So great was the force of their primitive weapons that a well-aimed missile could penetrate the armour of the day. Accuracy of aim was inculcated into the very young by heads of households, who followed the practice of lodging each boy's daily ration of food in the high branches of a tree, leaving him to bring it down by slingshot, or else go hungry.

It is from these redoubtable marksmen that the Balearics are named, *ballein* being the Greek word for 'to sling.' It is clear that the name was in common usage in the second century BC, at the time of Quintus Cecilius Metullus, the Roman consul who conquered the islands about 123 BC as part of his operations against the pirates who persistently harried the sea routes between Rome and Spain. So critical to the Roman economy was this victory that when Metullus returned to the capital in triumph he was endowed with the title of Balearicus. His method of neutralising the firepower of the natives had been to set up giant screens of rawhide along the gunwales of his ships, so as to prevent the penetration of the missiles into the ships' timbers, and thus reduce casualties. According to Diodorus Siculus, the Majorcans of the day were also greatly addicted to wine. However, this does not seem to have affected the accuracy of the slingers' aim. Apparently wine was already being produced in such quantity in Majorca that it could be exported to Rome, though no comparable quantity of olives and their by-products was achieved until Roman settlers were introduced to the island, bringing with them their traditional horticultural skills.

Roman colonisation began with Metullus in the period of the *Pax Romana*. He imported 3000 Roman settlers, and established colonies at Palmaria (Palma) and Pollentia (Pollensa) on Majorca, while from the evidence of sunken galleys and a wealth of recovered amphorae it can be deduced that there were further settlements at Puerto de Campos and nearby Colonia Sant Jordi on the south coast. By the first century AD when the island became part of the Roman province of Tarragonensis administered from Tarragona on the Spanish mainland, the total population numbered some 30,000. But it was not until AD 211 that the emperor Caracalla extended Roman citizenship to all people dwelling within the imperial frontiers. Later, in AD 401, the Balearics achieved provincial status, separate administratively from the Spanish provinces ruled by Rome.

In the meantime, during the latter stages of Roman influence, Christianity flourished under the suffragan bishop of Tarragona. Unfortunately, however, the islands possess singularly few traces of early ecclesiastical architecture. This is partly because succeeding conquerors of the Balearics showed a tendency to destroy or to allow to fall to ruin all evidence of cultures which preceded their own, and also because no natural cataclysm such as earthquake or volcanic eruption occurred to preserve them for discovery by posterity, as at Pompeii or Salamis on the island of Cyprus. The exceptions are the megalithic monuments, which were wholly resistant to weather, and whose materials were too ponderous to be put to any practical contemporary use. At all events, the foundations of two triple-naved basilicas probably dating from the early third century, are all that have survived in Majorca: one at Sa Carrotja in Porto Cristo, and the other at Son Pereto, near Manacor; and there is another and similar church on the south coast of Minorca which existed unnoticed until as late as 1951.

Christianity itself withstood the depradations of the Vandals, the ruthless band of migrants from the Baltic who passed through central Europe and Spain, and who raided the islands in 425 and 426, wreaking the havoc and destruction which has been encapsulated in their name for all time. Deliverance was to come from the east, in the person of Belisarius, the great Byzantine general who served Justinian, ruler of the Eastern Roman Empire from his capital at Constantinople. He harried the Vandals by sea and by land, finally routing them in North Africa in AD 533. The Balearic islands were formally incorporated into the Byzantine empire in the following year.

However, the protective power of the Byzantines did not hold for more than two centuries. There were early signs that their civilisation was fated to be overwhelmed by the Moslems along the whole length of the southern shores of the Mediterranean, reaching west to North Africa and across the Straits of Gibraltar to Spain. A new religion and a new culture were simultaneously introduced to the conquered lands. As early as 707 and 708 Arab naval forces operating in the western Mediterranean had launched raids against the Balearic islands, to withdraw with hauls of booty in the form of captive Christians, whatever shipping happened to be in port, as well as treasure and other loot. These raids set a pattern which was to persist over a great number of years. Initially the Arabs as they gathered strength were satisfied to plunder the islands repeatedly, and to draw from them whatever was to hand by way of slaves, provisions and armament. The territorial prize could be left as a preserve ready for some future picking, considering that despite the strategic vulnerability of the islands there was no other Mediterranean power strong enough first to seize and then to garrison them. This state of affairs continued during the Arabs' spectacular conquest of Spain, which began in 711 and was completed within five years. The offshore islands maintained their insecure *status quo* throughout the eighth century.

In 797 Charlemagne despatched an expedition against Barcelona, which had been captured by the Moors in 716. That city did not return to Christian hands until 801, when taken by Louis the Pious, Charlemagne's son, and incorporated into the Frankish realm with the Count of Barcelona its titular head. It is worth remembering, when considering twentieth century Spanish politics, that Barcelona became virtually independent from the rest of Spain in 865, though with nominal French suzerainty. In the meantime Charlemagne's earlier expedition, which entailed sending a fleet to protect the Balearics against continuing Saracen raids, had provoked the Moors into a series of reprisals, culminating in 848 in one of the most punitive of all which was mounted against Majorca by the Emirate of Cordova. Finally, in 902, the island of Majorca was occupied by the Emirate, and later superseded by the Caliphate of Cordova. As distinct from using the Balearics, the Moors had taken them over, somewhat belatedly. But though the sway of the Moors in Spain held firm, their rule began to suffer from internal political strife. As soon as the power of the Caliphate showed signs of waning, the Wali of Denia, who had been appointed Governor of Majorca, proclaimed himself to be the independent ruler of the offshore islands. His regimen was supplanted in 1015 by that of the Wali of Morthada, who converted the entire island of Majorca into a pirate stronghold from which he could ravage the coasts and shipping of Catalonia, France and Italy. These operations struck dread into the hearts of inhabitants of the northerly seaboard of the western Mediterranean, who as yet had found no counter-solution to the phenomenal conquests of the Arab overlords whose armies had swarmed over such a large proportion of the known world, from the Middle East to North Africa, and finally penetrated into Europe to make much of Spain and Catalonia their own.

And yet the Balearics appear to have reaped some benefit from their capture. Instead of being repeatedly subjected to vicious raids by outlandish infidels, they were now afforded protection. In fact over a period the internal affairs of Moorish Spain achieved a degree of peaceful settlement which was reflected in its dependencies. The usurped Spanish provinces became united in an Arab state known as Al-Andaluz where, rather surprisingly but true to Moslem teaching, religious tolerance was practised, so that Christians, Moors and Jews learned to live together, developing their own skills and following their professions, thus becoming socially interdependent. The Christians of the islands, who came to be known as Mozarabs, specialised in agriculture, and developed the land by terracing and irrigation, making the best of traditional Roman and Moorish techniques. Jews tended to channel their skills into medicine, law, trade and learning. Intermarriage between Christians and Moslems was not disallowed, nor was conversion from one faith to another, though the Jewish population elected to remain true to its own race and religion, so that the trend was for them to congregate in distinct quarters of important towns, as in Palma. It is an index of religious tolerance on the part of the Moslem rulers of the islands, who were first known as merciless raiders, that there was little interference in Christian worship after the first years of settlement. In 1058 the Bishop of Barcelona was acknowledged as the head of the Church in the Balearics, which were declared an independent emirate in 1075.

All the same, in spite of the relative peace which prevailed in lands overrun by the Moors, it could not be expected that the European Christian powers would ever acknowledge their right of conquest. A Christian power bloc was building up. In 1114-15 Pisa combined with the Catalans in a crusade headed by Count Berenguer III of Barcelona in mounting a fleet of 500 ships and 70,000 men to invade Majorca. Palma, which at that date went by the Arab name of Medina Mayurca, was taken, and its walls razed. At the end of the day it became known that though 30,000 Christians held captive during the siege had been liberated, many more were unaccounted for. In reprisal, all the Moslems of Palma were massacred before the Christian expedition withdrew from positions it was powerless to hold indefinitely against the Moors from across the water.

An uneasy situation prevailed in the islands with the reinstallation of Moorish rule, which by now had become beset by internecine strife leading first to the break-up of Al-Andaluz or Moorish Spain into *taifas* of principalities, to be followed by seizure of power by the Almoravide dynasty, which was among the most fanatical of Moslem sects, recruited from among the Berbers of North Africa. Though ground on the mainland was being lost to Castile, the offshore islands, key positions in overall strategy, settled down fairly equably once more after the Almoravides had proclaimed independent sovereignty in 1127. External threats were also minimized by the Italian city states defying papal injunctions, by continuing to trade with the Moors, so that the position of other Christian powers in the Mediterranean was undermined. This was particular evident in Palma, which had become a place of refuge for Christians in revolt against overlords of their own faith elsewhere.

The Moors dominated the islands for four centuries, during

the latter years of which they were ruled by the Almohads, a Moslem dynasty born in 1159 of a religious revival centred on Marrakesh. Their avowed aim was to command the whole of Spain as well as North Africa—an expansionist policy which exceeded previous concepts. Ten years fighting on the mainland had reunited Andalusia, which had been weakened by division into principalities; a splendid court was established in Seville, and a strong Castilian army was defeated at Alarcos.

Though the Balearic islands were now settled, they maintained their reputation as strongholds from which to harry and destroy Christian shipping, and to repel potential invaders of the Spanish mainland. It was this continuing role which led directly to events which more than any others shaped the islands, historically and politically, giving them their present-day characteristics.

The Christian kingdoms of Aragon and Catalonia had been united in 1150. At the age of five Jaime I came to the throne, with the resounding titles of Count of Barcelona, King of Aragon, and Lord of Montpellier. He had grown up to lurid reports of encounters at sea between the Moors of the Balearic islands and the Christians of Catalonia and Roussillon, but during the year he reached his majority a similar tale affected him even more critically. A galley belonging to the Arab emir of Majorca was seized and carried off from an Ibizan port, to be followed by the inevitable reprisal, when two Catalan ships were taken by the Arabs. By accident or by design, on 16 November 1228 the youthful king was invited to a banquet in Tarragona, to find that the table was loaded with Majorcan delicacies, and all the talk was of the rich potential of the islands lying so close offshore. As was the intention, Jaime's enthusiasm was fired, with the result that before he departed from the festivities he had determined to put defensive policies behind him by delivering the Balearics from the Arabs. Support was forthcoming from the Church, who gave the plans the official stamp as a Crusade.

The invasion force was ready by September 1229. It consisted of more than 500 ships, most of which were contributed by Tarragona and Barcelona, as the most interested parties, but some came from as far afield as Genoa, Marseilles and Narbonne. The Aragonese nobles alone held back, their given reason being that their primary and longer-term objective must be a mainland operation aimed at the reconquest of the Moorish kingdom of Valencia. As was the custom in those times, the nobles and feudal landowners of Jaime's dominions participated in the Balearic enterprise on the understanding that they would be individually rewarded by grants of land proportionate to their contribution in manpower and armament.

The story of the successful invasion belongs to the more detailed history of Majorca, related to places, districts and buildings which are still to be seen. Palma, which bore the brunt of the attack,· was sacked on the last day of 1229, though the total capitulation of the island by the Moors did not take place until 1232, the same year that the Moslem ruler of Minorca acknowledged Jaime I as ruler, and became his vassal. That island was not formally annexed until 1286, in the reign of Alfonso III, King of Aragon. Ibiza was captured in 1235.

With some exceptions, there is disappointingly little surviving evidence of the Moorish domination of the islands to remind present day visitors of that civilised though alien culture. After the defeat of the Moors there followed a rebirth of all three islands which is today visible in their architecture, systems of land cultivation and tenure, and the social structure, all of which combine to place them among the most popular of holiday grounds.

The thirteenth century was an age of power politics, during which time the kingdoms of France and Aragon competed for territory. When in 1256 Louis IX of France, who became known to the world as St Louis, laid claim to Barcelona and its dependencies, which included the Balearics, King Jaime I of Aragon, who had taken on the additional title of Jaime I of Majorca, renounced his rights in most of what is now south-west France, though still retaining several provinces, including Roussillon and Montpellier. Louis reciprocated by withdrawing his claim to Catalonia, and, by implication, to the Balearics.

Upon the death of Jaime I in 1276 it was discovered that he had willed his Spanish possessions—Aragon, Catalonia and his rights in Valencia—to his elder son, Pedro III, while the Balearics were to become the portion of the younger boy, who then assumed the title of King Jaime II of Majorca. This division of the realm caused great bitterness between the brothers, who immediately formed conflicting alliances: Pedro with the Sicilians, who were in the ascendant as a Mediterranean power, and Jaime with the French. Majorca, which at first had been overjoyed at having its own king, very soon lost much of its enthusiasm, chiefly because Jaime II elected to spend most of his time in France, at Perpignan, which he named as his capital. He was much criticised for leaving the conduct of Majorcan affairs to the nobles who had fought with his father and achieved the reconquest. This situation was taken advantage of by his brother, King Pedro III of Aragon, who set about planning an invasion in order to enlarge his domain. And though the enterprise was delayed by the King of Aragon's death it was taken up by his son, Alfonso III, who succeeded him in 1285.

Palma was captured without substantial loss of life or damage, though greater resistance was put up in the country, notably by the royal castles of Alaro, Pollensa and Santueri, to the north and east of the capital. Alfonso proclaimed himself king of Majorca, and went on to take Minorca in 1287, but died four years later, whereupon he was succeeded by his brother, confusingly another Jaime, who had become King of Sicily. However in 1295 the Papacy decreed that Majorca be restored to its own King Jaime II, who would become a vassal of the kingdom of Aragon, and this was done. From that date onward until his death in 1311 Jaime redeemed himself in Majorcan eyes by identifying himself completely with the interests of his island kingdom, with the result that there was a noticeable resurgence of commerce based on the founding of inland towns and markets, stabilisation of agriculture and trade, and the strengthening of coastal defences.

The next Catalan ruler of Majorca, King Sancho, was a sufferer from severe bouts of asthma, which prevented him from fully participating in the government of his country. He spent most of his time away from his capital, preferring the salubrious heights of Valldemossa, where he built himself a castle. Nevertheless, he contrived to keep on good terms with the kings of Aragon and France. During his reign, from 1311 to 1324, trade continued to prosper, encouraged by the construction of an important merchant fleet. The flaw was that so much money was involved that these capital developments took up all available resources, so that there was delay in acquiring and equipping a navy to protect the new trade routes. In this respect Majorca had to rely precariously upon the good offices of friendly states.

Sancho had no direct heir. When he died in 1324 he was succeeded by his nine-year-old nephew, who became Jaime III. His uncle Philip headed a regency council. The boy's accession was violently opposed by Jaime II of Aragon. Nevertheless all went fairly well until the young king attained his majority and assumed sovereign powers. Though he succeeded to a great extent in protecting his country and its trade against piracy, he alienated European sovereigns, particularly arousing the hatred of his brother-in-law, who as Pedro IV had become king of Aragon. This antagonism was translated into practical terms: after landing on Majorca in 1343 Pedro proclaimed the incorporation of the island into his own kingdom. At the same time he seized the Majorcan king's Catalan possessions, though in one instance Jaime III forestalled him by selling Montpellier to France, so that funds might be available for a return to his island kingdom.

By 1349 Jaime III had gathered together what forces he could afford, and made a landing on the north coast of Majorca. But the invasion was ill-fated: Jaime was killed and his army defeated. He was to be the last independent king of Majorca, though his 11-year-old son, who was wounded and taken prison in battle outside Lluchmayor, was allowed to survive. He never fulfilled nationalist hopes that he would regain the throne to rule as King Jaime IV.

Majorcan commerce went into decline in the middle of the fourteenth century. Several factors militated against continued prosperity—heavy taxation was levied by Aragon, and as a satellite of the larger kingdom the island was denied mercantile initiative. Trade with the Italian city states flagged, and very soon the only interchange was with the Spanish mainland. Further developments contributed to economic recession including the capture of Constantinople by the Turks in 1453 which put an end to international trade in the eastern Mediterranean and meant that fewer ships passed through the Straits of Gibraltar. The discovery of the New World and its untold riches did nothing to compensate Majorca, because though Spain had been unified in 1469 by the marriage of Isabella of Castile to King Ferdinand of Aragon, the terms of the Queen's will precluded Aragon, Catalonia and the Balearics from engaging in trade with the Americas. This restriction was not lifted until 1778, by which time Castile had profited immeasurably at the expense of its dependencies. Another factor which contributed to the decline in Majorcan commerce was the success of Portuguese navigators in establishing a trade route around the Cape of Good Hope, which again put the Balearics off the map. And when the Moors were finally expelled from Spain, traffic with North Africa virtually came to an end, since the intervening seas became infested with predatory corsairs. In fact, the golden ages of commerce and navigation were over as far as the islands were concerned. Industry and commerce suffered from this contraction of markets, and this led to agrarian troubles. Much hardship and loss of life was inflicted by the Spanish Inquisition.

Majorca and Minorca frequently found themselves ranged

on opposite political sides. When there was a mainland rising in Catalonia against Spain in 1461 Majorca remained loyal, whereas the Minorcans espoused the rebel cause. Similar divergences occurred during the War of the Spanish Succession, between 1702 and 1713. Though the Spanish majority favoured the French claimant, Philip of Anjou, grandson of King Louis XIV of France, the Catalans and Majorcans supported the claim of Charles, the Austrian Archduke of Hapsburg. Britain fought against the combined Spanish and French forces, since she feared the build-up of power in the alliance of these two nations. She intervened by capturing Gibraltar in 1704 and Minorca, with its two great natural harbours, in 1708. In the same year a British naval force landed on Ibiza and received that island's submission, as well as effecting a landing at Palma, where no more than token resistance was encountered. But Minorca was the only one of the three islands to be of practical value to Britain, to be used essentially as a naval base. It was to remain in British hands for a century, interrupted by two breaks.

When the Spanish succession was settled in 1713 by the Treaty of Utrecht, and after Philip of Anjou had renounced his claims to the throne, the fate of Catalonia was in the balance, and with it the destiny of the islands. For a time there was talk of the creation of an independent republic—echoes of which persist to the present day. The British, fearing détente between France and Austria, offered to act as guarantors of Catalan integrity, but withdrew this undertaking when it was discovered that the Catalans were to be accorded preferential trading rights with the Indies, which would infringe British trading interests. Meanwhile the Catalan population of Barcelona, supported by British naval units, continued to oppose assault by combined French and Castilian troops. But when Barcelona fell in 1714, Majorca still remained loyal to the Catalan cause. The consequence was that Philip of Anjou sent an expedition against the island. He seized Alcudia and Felanitx, and then besieged Palma for 17 days. Majorca became a province of Spain in 1716.

Minorca remained in British hands until 1756, when it was ignominiously captured in a surprise attack by the French in the course of the Seven Years' War. However, the island was to be returned to England in 1768 under the Treaty of Paris in exchange for the Philippines and Cuba, both of which had been wrested from Spain in 1756. Then, with the connivance of France, Minorca was to fall to Spain less than 20 years later, to be held by them until 1782 when Britain entered into her third period of rule, which was terminated by the Treaty of Amiens in 1802.

During all these troubles, Majorca managed to remain on the sidelines, though it was evident that wherever a choice had to be made her sympathies lay more with Catalan interests than with those of Spain, and that this nationalist feeling was mirrored in the direct divergence of opinion in the policitical affiliations of the two principal islands. In the Spanish Civil War of 1936 Minorca declared for the Republican cause, whereas Majorca put up little resistance to being used as a Nationalist base by Italy and Germany. Feeling still runs high on the subject, so that the civil war, and its atrocities on both sides, is still an unsuitable subject for discussion in guide books or in conversation when visiting the islands.

1 Majorca Today

The first glimpse of an island where one is to stay some days or weeks is always an exciting experience, especially when it is not too large to visualise as a whole. These days the majority of visitors to Majorca arrive by air, touching down at the modern and very busy airport a short distance to the east of Palma. With any luck, if the flight is in daylight, the plane will have come in over the north-western tip of the island, at the extremity of a range of steep mountains which form a rampart between the fertile interior of the island and the sea separating the Balearics from mainland Spain.

This first impression gives an idea of things to come, and places to explore. Perhaps most dramatic of all is the island's mountainous region, which stretches from Cape Formentor in the north to the island of Dragonera in the south-west, and which is broken only by a few high passes though which roads and one light railway thread and occasionally burrow their way. The eagle-haunted crags, the monasteries, the terraced cultivation of the foothills, the rock formations—all these sights can later be appreciated and, possibly, explored from ground level. And there will be bonus glimpses of the occasional fishing village in places where the cliffs do not drop sheer to the sea, and unbelievable panoramas from coast roads weaving serpentine courses high above sea level. This is the most spectacular region of Majorca, and at the same time, the most inhospitable. Yet for many years this coast and these mountains and their once secret villages have been the refuge of foreign artists, writers and other expatriates whose work and tastes incline them towards the simple life and settings of such natural grandeur. The shores provide little scope for major development; they are frequented mainly by day visitors, many of them making use of escorted tours.

The Bay of Palma lies immediately to the south, bounded on one side by rocky headlands and on the other by level land and, eventually, by low, regular cliffs. Spreading out on either side of the city there are a series of beaches which have invited the growth of a holiday industry comparable to that of the Costa Brava. Here are the serried ranks of hotels, apartment blocks and other amenities known rather unattractively in Spanish as *urbanizacions,* which have become an accepted feature of the landscape.

Palma de Mallorca, to give the capital city its true name, stands at the very heart of its bay, and holds a great attraction for people of all kinds staying elsewhere on the coasts, just as it has always done for foreign merchants and adventurers, as well as for the natives of the lesser-known districts of the central plain who come to the capital to sell their goods or their services.

The entire coastline is subject to development, except where nature has ordained otherwise, but generally speaking, the further east one travels from Palma the better the chance of finding some intimate resort complete with quayside haunts, local colour and expansion which is not at odds with the environment. And in the east, though on a very much smaller scale, there is another line of mountains—or hills rather—which similarly run from north-east to south-west. This is the quieter side of the island, with attractions in the form of castles, religious sanctuaries and, above all, caves of almost unbelievable grandeur.

The northern shore which extends from Cape Formentor in two great arcs is different again. The sheltered waters below the high mountains led to this part of the island being settled by invaders, notably the Romans. Their Pollentia, which we call Pollensa, and Alcudia have between them a theatre carved out of the rock and an attractive small bridge over a seasonal watercourse as reminders of the Roman period. This coast has been the last to challenge the developers, for the reason that much of it consisted of the Albufera, a region of marshland beloved of wildfowlers and conservationists which has done its best to defy reclamation schemes, but which continues to be threatened by the human appetite for expansion. Between these marshes and the rocky, almost roadless north-east tip of the island, new *urbanizacions* on a grand scale have sprung up to complete the dispersal of holidaymakers around the perimeter of the island.

It is impossible to consider the Majorcan coasts without associating them with mass tourism and the changes it imposes both on the landscape and among the native population. Certainly these changes cannot be wholeheartedly deplored, because not only is pleasure given to tens of thousands of visitors annually, but it must also be remembered that the growth of what has become a major industry has transformed a recently impoverished island into one which hums with activity, and caters for visitors throughout 12 months of the year. No one should begrudge the Majorcans this reversal of fortunes. In point of fact, tourism as a prime endeavour can be said to date from not much earlier than the beginning of the 1950s, since when there has been a marked improvement in the population's standard of living. In the past, because of the lack of opportunity at home, a great many of the islanders were forced to emigrate to South America and Cuba, as well as travelling, for seasonal work, to North Africa and, latterly, France. These days, more happily, the movement of population is largely limited to within the island itself. Workers drift in from remoter districts for employment in the building and service industries. Consequently the shift is to the capital and its resorts, while earnings filter back immediately to the villages, where they augment the proceeds of smallholdings.

Though oranges, vines and olives flourish in the foothills of the mountains, the bulk of agricultural and horticultural produce comes from the central plain which, incidentally, has a charm which might easily be overlooked by the visitor. This is for the most part a fertile region, some of it flat, and at other places swelling into shapely hills. Almonds are the most spectacular of its crops. In spite of the stress laid on the blossom in travel brochures, the reality is difficult to imagine, because we are too greatly conditioned by some beautiful but isolated specimens which flourish in our own suburban gardens. The Majorcan truth is far different: It is said that there are as many as 6,000,000 almond trees on the island, most of them in plantations, and that these contribute two-thirds of the almond production of the whole of Spain. 80% of the Majorcan crop is exported, which leaves ample for the appetisers and confectionery which add frills to staple foodstuffs. But statistics mean little when the reality can be seen, at its best in February, at which time the delicate trees, still without their pale foliage, burst into a froth of bloom which covers square miles at a time with what looks like a newly laundered lace coverlet. Large-scale planting was begun as early as 1765. Trees show a profit after seven years. Sweet almonds have pink blossom; the bitter variety white. August is the time of the harvesting of the crop, and even though production is on such a large scale the operation remains fairly primitive, and consists of shaking the almonds into sheets spread beneath the trees. Usually it is the task of women to cut away the velvety outer shells. The oil is extracted in mills under pressure, and is used chiefly for pharmaceutical and cosmetic purposes, while the residual hard inner shells can be burned as fuel.

Though there are exceptional districts close to Palma and around the Bay of Alcudia, not much of the land is owned by peasants. In fact, to date there has not been a great deal of departure from the traditional landholding practice. Large estates, reminiscent of the division of land among Jaime I's noble followers, are owned by important families while being farmed by tenants, sometimes on a shares system. Until the advent of the tourist industry the island was more than self-supporting, but these days substantial quantities of foodstuffs have to be brought in. Nevertheless, the variety of cereal crops, fruit and vegetables grown at home is very impressive, as may be seen in any local market, especially in Palma, where almost everything produced on the island is gathered under the roof of an enormous covered market which hums with activity. Otherwise, even if only as features of the landscape, the seasonal cultivations add immeasurably to the pleasures of cross-country expeditions. Citrus fruits, peaches and apricots follow almonds in the calendar of blossom; oranges are picked as they ripen instead of as a single crop. The corn harvest occurs in May and June; figs—grown in straight lines and carefully pruned—ripen in August, grapes in September, and olives in October. Then, to complete the cycle, ploughing begins with the first rains of autumn.

One of the fascinations disclosed by exploration of the countryside is that farming practices are often family affairs with a minimal use of machinery. Mules and horses are used for ploughing and harrowing. This is because the traditional practice of growing catch crops between lines of trees or even vines does not leave much room for manoeuvre by tractors pulling heavy implements. Cattle and sheep are not much in evidence, since it is more economic to stall-feed them. And because the boundaries between holdings are seldom stock-proof, nor even clearly defined, the animals which are put out to graze are usually spancelled or hobbled, and sometimes belled, and may have as attendant a man, woman or child, looking very biblical.

In the north, not far from the Albufera marshes, potatoes are the main crop, though a great many artichokes and other vegetables are also grown. Some districts here were once very rocky, but piles of stones have been collected into heaps in the course of land reclamation, as in the west of Ireland, where walls frequently cover a larger area of ground than the fields they enclose. There are also a great many windmills in this part of the island, used for pumping up underground water, or draining the surplus from the fringes of the marshes. In the context of irrigation, the advent of the Moors should be remembered with gratitude, because it was they who introduced their traditional system of *norias,* the technique whereby water was hauled to the surface and distributed by means of channels threading their way over a considerable area. They also brought palms and oranges to the islands, while their method of dry-stone walling, seen in its most expert form on the steep slopes of the west coast near Bañalbufar and Esporlas, is a feature of the island, every bit as delightfully characteristic, as the olives and vines said to have been introduced by the Romans.

Though Majorca is the largest of the Balearic islands it is one of the easiest to explore, due to a network of roads radiating in three directions from Palma, as though from a nerve centre. As to the south there is the sea with its own lanes, leading not only to Minorca, Ibiza, Spain and the outer world, but to nearer attractions, precipitous landing places and offshore islands—chief among which is Cabrera, near the south east tip of the island.

Majorca has a railway system besides excellent road communications. However, with one exception, passenger travel is not to be recommended either for speed or comfort. It is interesting to recall that the first stretch of line from Palma to Inca—the only one to be double-tracked—was British-built, and its rolling stock came from the Midlands. The opening ceremony took place in 1875. Subsequent extensions were built to La Puebla, then from Inca to Sineu at the very centre of the island, and later still to Manacor and Artá. Further branches serving Santañi and Felanitx were closed down in 1965 and 1967, one reason being a decline in rail traffic which dated from the 1936 Civil War, another being a modern revitalising road-building programme based on the recognition that losses on rail traffic and freight had unfortunately been built into the system because many towns and villages to be served were for historical reasons situated on elevated ground, whereas the stations serving them had to keep to the level, sometimes many miles distant.

However, to compensate for the shortcomings of the principal railway system, Majorca has one very special line: a railway journey which can be acclaimed as one of the highlights of a visit. The journey is from Palma to Soller on the west coast, with a few intermediate halts. The track climbs high into the mountain range before disappearing intermittently into tunnels blasted out of the hard core of the peaks. The inhabitants of Soller built their line from the considerable profits of their citrus trade. It was inaugurated in 1912. The first engine was made in Loughborough, Leicestershire, but this has now been replaced by diesels. The Palma terminus adjoins the ordinary railway station in the Plaza de España, and has a completely distinct quality. The rolling stock is delightfully antiquated in design—though not in standards of comfort or range of vision—the first-class carriages being particularly 'period', and provided with commodious armchairs. Leisurely progress though the suburbs passes into a sequence of many and varied forms of vegetation: mixed farming, orange groves, then olives, figs and pines in ascending sequence before the train reaches the first of its nine tunnels, thereafter emerging to magnificent views of the mountain peaks in steep descent to the sea, and far below eagle-eyed glimpses of Sóller and the bright green of citrus plantations.

Apart from opportunities for independent exploration, the island and every one of its famous places and beauty spots are particularly well served by coach excursions. Places on these can readily be booked at hotel reception desks, or through couriers attached to individual package tours. It is usual for coaches to call at a number of hotels in one resort soon after breakfast, and to pick up their complement of passengers, before setting off on a carefully organised programme which includes stops at market towns, monasteries, caves and harbours, according to direction. Time is always allowed for the consumption of a packed lunch, and for sightseeing, as well as for visits to certain factories given over to some local industry. In most cases these have a retail shop under the same roof. Perhaps the most popular are the distilleries, where sampling is run on a help-yourself basis. This method of seeing the island is better than nothing, though it should be understood that in spite of the services of well-intentioned multi-lingual guides there is little opportunity for leisurely exploration of the majority of halting-places, however interesting. Queues are unavoidable.

It must be admitted that in season Majorca is crowded, and that English people are not the only northerners to have chosen it as a playground. Accordingly, the tourist authorities have come to cater primarily for the masses. However, the climate is such that many of the off-peak months are preferable for a visit, especially an active one. February is the coldest month, with an average daytime temperature of 10·5°C, and July the warmest with 24·1°C. Records suggest that there will be 266 sunny days in each year, some 186 of these being between October and April. Another yardstick gives 5 hours of sun in winter, and more than 10 on summer days. There may be as many as 66 days on which rain falls, but the philosophical amongst us will welcome these if they do not run together, because of the magic effect even one heavy shower can have on surface vegetation, and eventually upon the island's produce, as well, of course, as on the supply of bath water for hundreds of hotels.

The people one encounters on inland travels and in many quarters of the towns, are far from typical Spaniards. Instead, they hark back racially to the time of the Catalan reconquest of the island under Jaime I, when the preponderance of settlers were Catalan. The Mallorquin language, which most of the islanders speak among themselves, is similar to the Catalan tongue such as continues to be spoken by the inhabitants of the north-eastern seaboard of Spain, spreading over into the French province of Roussillon on the far side of the Pyrenees. Though distinct from it, there is a resemblance to Provençal; these are, as it were, parallel tongues. However, visitors need not be alarmed: the official language is Spanish, and Castilian Spanish at that. Mallorquin incorporates a certain number of obviously Arabic words, particularly those which relate to agriculture, architecture, commerce or science—that is, appropriate to the crafts and professions in which the North African invaders excelled. A great many place names—Binisalem is one of them—are obviously Moorish, while others, notably those which end with an 'x', as in Andraitx, are exclusively Mallorquin.

It is also held that Catalan characteristics have persisted in the islanders to this day, so much so that Majorcans have never been regarded, nor see themselves, as Iberians or men from the peninsula. In the past they were referred to as Franks, and renowned as individualists. They made perspicacious traders and brave sailors, in contrast to the Castilians, who tended to be rather more dignified and content to stay at home. There is greater affinity with the Spaniards of Valencia, whose heredity also includes an admixture of Moorish blood. In this connection it may be recalled that Moorish influences lasted longer in the Balearics than they did on the mainland.

As well as meeting Majorcan people in the market places, shops, churches and villages, and amusing oneself by distinguishing foreign visitors from the expatriates of all nations, there is the occasional gipsy family to be reckoned with. But these colourful people have been greatly discouraged by the authorities, both because of their shiftlessness and their habit of pestering tourists on sidewalks and beaches. In fact, these Romanies are outcasts here more than in many other countries, and not very romantic either now that they have been directed into a suburban housing estate on the outskirts of Palma. The language they use, known as Cale, has been described as debased Spanish, though in fact it is polyglot, and is peppered with Greek, Hungarian, Romanian and Egyptian words.

The majority of Majorca's population are busy and cheerful people, who in less than one generation have adapted themselves to an influx of visitors unimaginable 30 years ago. They seem to work non-stop, and with good humour, probably aware that it is in their own interests to keep the tourist trade in gear throughout the year by means of holidays such as appeal to elderly people with time on their hands, and younger ones able to take a quick, flying off-season break. Terms compare most favourably with what would have to be spent on similar home holidays, even when the cost of flight is included. During the off-peak season coach tours, entertainments and a variety of indoor festivities at various hotels continue, the dual purpose being not only to win clients but also to keep staff in good shape and ready trained for months when they may expect greater pressure. Of course even though the winter climate is good compared with that of northern and central Europe, certain outdoor fixtures, as for instance bull-fighting, are strictly seasonal. But it will be discovered that the inhabitants of all three islands have a parallel, not so secret calendar of their own, to which they willingly admit anyone caring to participate.

As in mainland Spain, the majority of Majorcan festivals follow the Christian pattern of Saints' and other feast days, and are celebrated with great gusto. For instance the arrival of the Magi, when they disembark with their traditional gifts after Christmas, is in the form of a seaborne landing illuminated by firework displays. St Anthony's feast day, celebrated on the 16th and 17th of January at the inland town of La Puebla, is enlivened by troupes of singers and dancers, known engagingly as *los cançoners del camp,* who perform to the accompaniment of tambourines and drums as well as some fascinating old-world hurdy gurdies known as *ximbombes.* Animals are brought into the town on the second day, resplendent in decorated harness, to receive the blessing of their patron saint. At the same time masked youngsters, dressed as demons and miming the part, add colour and gaiety to the festival.

Holy Week, of course, is a solemn period in all Roman

Catholic countries, and Palma celebrates it with a particularly impressive procession on Maundy Thursday. Various religious fraternities whose origins date from the medieval guilds, gather together first outside the city's principal hospital. Their members are clad in penitential robes, complete with the macabre hoods worn by the Inquisitors. Barefooted, and dragging chains behind them, they walk in procession through the streets, bearing litters which depict each of the Stations of the Cross. Ceremonial drums roll, and the populace carries candles. The last group but one bears aloft the statue of the Virgin Mary adorned with Easter lilies, preceding the representation of Christ Crucified. Following them comes the Mayor of Palma supported by other civic dignitaries, all in evening dress. This is one of the rare occasions when Majorcan women may be seen wearing the graceful Spanish mantilla. The procession takes its time before coming to a halt outside the Ayuntamiento, the beautiful seventeenth century Town Hall in the Plaza Cort, where a platform has been erected. Here the Christ is received by the Captain of the Balearics, come in ceremony from the Almudaina Palace, and supported by every other martial and civic notable. The people press forward to lay flowers at the feet of the Christ.

Then during the last week of June, on the Feast of St Peter, who is the patron saint of fishermen, festivities again take to the water. Alcudia is a good place to be on that day, or Andraitx, or even Esporlas, though the latter is in the mountains, and specialises in country sports and the entertainments known by the generic Spanish name of *verbenas*.

Feasts special to Majorca include that of Santa Catalina Tomás, a native-born saint much reverenced by country people. Her day is celebrated by music and dancing, while youths carrying pitchers are beset by 'demons' hellbent on breaking the pottery to pieces. Decorated chariots convey tableaux of the saints who are believed to have appeared to Santa Catalina. These are escorted by nuns and novices from the convent of Santa Magdalena of Palma. The festivities take place early in September in the village of Santa Margarita, inland from the Bay of Alcudia, but Santa Catalina is also honoured on 16 July in Palma, when a cavalcade enters the city and the occasion is shared with the Virgen del Carmen. Most of the fun and ceremonial centres round the port, where there is a sea-borne procession. Then the feast of St James, later in the month, is widely celebrated with great fervour, and sports, fairs and sometimes bullfights are staged in country towns such as Muro, Santañi, La Puebla and Felanitx.

The small town of Petra, which is the birthplace of Fray Junipero Serra, the founder of the Californian missions, celebrates a Feast of Almonds on 11 February, an occasion planned to coincide with Abraham Lincoln's birthday, making a double festivity for the American colony. Many country festivals have an esoteric pagan connotation, as for instance celebrations linked with the various harvests. Villafranca de Bonany stages a mammoth Melon Feast where the implications of fertility are inescapable, and competitors vie in producing not only the best and largest melon but also slogans and poems extolling the virtues of that luscious fruit. It almost goes without saying, too, that Binisalem, as the centre of the red wine industry, stages its own bibulous festival towards the end of September.

Historical pageants are perhaps the most spectacular of Majorcan annual events, and the most colourful of them celebrate the island's deliverance from Moorish oppression. On 31 December, to mark the day at the close of 1229 when King Jaime I first set foot ashore west of Palma, the staff which is actually part of the original royal standard is borne in procession through the streets to the music of brass bands. In May the town and port of Soller, on the west coast, lays on exciting enactments of the landing there of the Moors in 1651, and their violent repulse, while the battle is commemorated in more ecclesiastical terms on the Feast of Nuestra Señora de la Victoria.

But the catalogue of feasts, fairs, pageants and processions is too extensive for full details to be given here, especially as some of them are subject to slight variation from year to year. Happily a special booklet is issued yearly by the local Tourist Office, setting out nearly as many venues as there are days in the year, and applying to all the Balearic islands. At various other times, and scheduled for the convenience of coach parties, special folk dancing displays are given by country folk in native costume. Their dances include *boleros*, *copeos* and the unique Majorca *jotas Mateixas*, which may be accompanied by drums, fifes, bagpipes and sometimes even an ingenious one-man band.

Parallel to this wealth of folklore runs modern life. Tennis, golf and all forms of water sports are ready to hand. Enquiry at any hotel desk will produce local information. Actually the choice is so great that it is really best to say what is unavailable or impractical. Game fishing is out, because tuna are of no great size in this part of the Mediterranean, though fishing trips, alone or accompanied, in search of lesser breeds are easy to arrange. A great deal of the shooting is preserved for landowners, though arrangements may be made for visiting guns, as for instance those wishing to go wildfowling in the Albufera marshes. Gaming tables may be introduced as a result of official relaxation. And horse-trotting races take place on the outskirts of Palma at the Son Pardo Hippodrome on Sunday afternoons, while that stadium is likely to have doubled up that very morning as a speedway track. Manacor also boasts a trotting track. At both these places betting is on *pari-mutuel* lines, similar to the Tote, and there are no bookmakers. There is also a very special game called Jai-Alai, played in what resembles a fives court, where spectators are seated at one end. Great dexterity is used in manipulating the *cesta*, the curved basket strapped to each player's wrist which is used for catching and throwing the ball at speed. The majority of professionals engaged in this sport are Basques, a fact which is explained by the game's resemblance to the regional game of *pelota*.

Visitors unable or reluctant to explore the island in search of culture and entertainment are recommended to sample these at the Pueblo Español of Palma de Mallorca. This is a large touristic complex at the western edge of the capital. Though it is wholly modern, great pains have been taken to present various facets of the island's resources, entertainment, wining and dining and examples of its monumental arts. The various entertainments are diverse and well staged, and usually appreciated by the members of the various congresses which are accommodated in a magnificent purpose-built palace cheek by jowl with a modern outdoor 'Roman' theatre.

Although it will probably always attract its share of hostile debate it must be conceded nevertheless, that bull-fighting is very popular. Palma actually possesses the third largest bullring in Spain, and it seats some 14,000 spectators. The season is from 1 April until the end of October. For those who are interested, a few hints will not come amiss: book ahead, either through your hotel or the Bar Rincon Taurino in the Plaza Mayor in the centre of the city. Arrange transport in advance, either by taxi or coach, or else you will find yourself without. Choose your seats carefully according to season, bearing in mind that the ring is divided into segments, of which 1, 2 and 3 are in the shade (*sombra*) and are the most expensive, and 5, 6 and 7 are in full sunlight (*sol*), while 4 and 8 get half and half as the day progresses. All seats are reserved, and probably newcomers uncertain of their reaction to gore should not sit too close to the front. Hiring of cushions is to be recommended, as seats are hard, and these cushions *should not* be hurled into the arena in moments of passion and excitement, as might be popularly supposed. Above the seats there are boxes, and higher still a gallery the cheapest area of all, known as the *andanada*.

Apart from bullfighting, which is more properly classified as an art form, football is the most important spectator sport. Usually the island's team plays in the second division of Spanish football, though with occasional excursions into the first division. The game is played in the enormous Luis Sitjar Stadium in Palma, and on Sunday afternoons elsewhere on the island. Important matches are televised.

Eating out abroad is always an entertaining occupation. Most Majorcan restaurants are located in town centres, where they spill over on to the pavements, and of course some of the best and most intimate are to be found on seaside promenades and quays. There are a few exceptional establishments on certain scenic routes, such as the north-western coast road, where wayside laybys, built as *miradors* for appreciation of the view, may have excellent cafés, perched like eyries above sheer precipices. A useful provision for visitors on a restricted budget, are the special picnic areas attached to regular restaurants in many of the popular resorts. These have tables, chairs and shade, and people may bring their own packed lunches to eat at their leisure, at the price of whatever drinks they care to order by waiter service.

Majorcan restaurateurs habitually make certain concessions to northern tastes, both in the menu and the methods of cooking. Mealtimes, though elastic, do not follow the normal mainland Spanish pattern. Luncheons are served at our conventional midday times, though late arrivals are never frowned upon. However, the late dinner hours of 10 pm or after, *de rigueur* in Spain, and which fret English appetites into consumption of an undue quantity of *tapas* or succulent hors d'oeuvres with their drinks, no longer prevail, and hotel meals are served at what Britons regard as civilised hours. Even the fish and chip shops and their German equivalents which dole out *wurst* or hotdogs are apt to close down soon after midnight.

Typical Majorcan and Spanish food, which make the most of local produce, is excellent, and increasingly these dishes figure as optional on package tour hotel menus. Even so, chefs have learnt to use a light hand with the olive oil, which is a common ingredient in their cooking, even of soups. Majorca, in fact, has a reputation for good soup, and one known simply as *la sopa Mallorquina* is based on lightly fried vegetables in a sauce made of their own juices which is finally poured over very thin slices of bread. This soup can be of a degree of thickness which makes it worthy to be eaten as a substantial course. Fish soups are usually given body by the addition of rice, but otherwise they vary considerably—as for instance in the use of saffron. Indeed, fish is plentiful, and invariably tastefully presented either in its own right or in made-up dishes such as *coca,* a pie baked in the oven and smothered with a mixture of local fish and vegetables. *Zarzuela de Mariscos* is an imaginative and much grander dish of clams, mussels, shrimps and other shellfish, together with flaked white fish, stewed with tomatoes, almonds, herbs, garlic, wine and with a final dollop of brandy. Of all Mediterranean fish, fresh sardines—usually grilled—are the most popular, as well as being the least expensive; crustacea, such as lobsters, crayfish, scampi and even prawns being scarce because of an almost insatiable demand for export, are the most expensive. They may be selected live from a tank in full view of customers, thus guaranteeing their freshness, before being weighed and priced. In this way the cost is established in advance. They are usually broiled, *à la planche,* and served hot. Fried squid and octopus are more plebeian fare, and are not as rubbery as their nature suggests, though it should be remembered that when cooked in their own ink squid have a distinctive flavour, not to everyone's taste. Eels usually appear in *espinagada,* a spicy pie. Almost every main course in cheaper restaurants is apt to be smothered in tomato sauce, though not of the bottled variety.

Tasty meat dishes include *lechona,* which is roast sucking pig. Similarly the baby lamb is delicious. Interesting culinary use is made of herbs and spices. Kidneys (*riñones*) braised in sherry make an interesting main course, as does the intriguing *frito Mallorquin,* the mixed fry which usually includes *sesos* or brains as well as other succulent and unidentifiable ingredients. Then there is *tumbet,* the Majorcan equivalent of the French *ratatouille,* made of a combination of Mediterranean vegetables, such as aubergines, peppers, courgettes and tomatoes 'melted' in oil. The difference is that the local version contains cubed potatoes, and is therefore more filling. Pizzas come in a wealth of colours, sizes and decorations according to the expertise of individual chefs, though black olives and anchovies are the most favoured garnishes. Poultry is plentiful and flavoursome, since chickens are seldom battery produced. They are served either plain roast or in made-up dishes with other vegetables. The traditional chicken stew is called *escaladun.*

Picnickers would be well advised to provide themselves with *sobrasada,* which is a cooked sausage more likely to be to English taste than some others among the bewildering variety hanging in delicatessen shops. Otherwise they may order giant sandwiches, called *pampoli*, made from hunks of crusty bread spread with oil and filled with tomatoes, ham and other goodies. Plainer sandwiches are called *bocadillos*. Then, as a natural part of emergency rations, there is fruit according to season. This needs little advertisement, since it is to be seen growing all over the island, and piled in mounds in the markets. Oranges, figs, peaches and nectarines are superb. Almonds—plain, salted or sugared—are on sale everywhere, but seem to be surprisingly expensive considering they are one of the island's principal products. Pastries must not be forgotten. *Ensaimadas,* richly iced and round, may be eaten for breakfast, and can also assume gigantic proportions when gift-wrapped for festive occasions. Another 'must' is *turron,* a nougat of satisfying richness which is usually imported from the mainland, but could well be manufactured on the island.

The choice of an *aperitif* is a ritual which adds considerably to any respite in sightseeing or other activity. There is also a good choice of fruit drinks and minerals, amongst which are the ubiquitous colas. Beware of tap water, even in small quantities. This is no fad, and it is wise to keep a bottle of mineral water on one's hotel table, as well as in the bedroom. One of the most popular between-meal drinks, borrowed from Spain, appears to be *cuba libre,* which quite simply is a mixture of white rum and coca cola, well iced. The locally produced drink goes by the name of *palo,* and is flavoured with nutshells, themselves owning the invidious Spanish name of *cascara.* This potion is best sampled warily among the other liqueurs and aperitifs which may be drawn from the wood in the various *cuevas* or cellars attached to various distilleries in the wine-making districts, and for which no charge is made. In fact when coach parties arrive on the scene there is a veritable free-for-all. When drinking brandy it is advisable to stick to approved makes such as Fundador, Soberando and Veterano—the latter advertised by giant cut-outs of a bull which looms over many a skyline. Beer strikes one as expensive. The best rum is the Bacardi of cocktail fame. Spanish gin and whisky vary in quality and price, but all are of course very much cheaper than brands brought in from abroad. As for wine, though a large quantity is made on the island, this is still insufficient to meet demand, so that a great deal is imported. In spite of this, it is worthwhile seeking out the local produce, bearing in mind that Binisalem, Consell and Inca—all on the Palma-Alcudia highway—are the main centres for red wines, and

Felanitx for whites. Imported champagnes are classified as *dulce* (sweet), *seco* (dry) and *semi-seco* or *brut*. Besides being palatable in its own right, even the cheapest champagne makes exhilarating cocktails with the addition of Spanish brandy. Another cooling drink which is mixed before being brought to the dining-table, is *sangria,* as served in Spain. This is best described as a form of cup, stronger than it appears to be, made of red wine—hence the bloody appellation—fruit juice, brandy and/or champagne, with slices of many coloured fruit floating gaily in it.

Pavement lounging and shopping go well together. A great many objects of interest and practical value may be brought home from Majorca, as well as the assortment of fresh market vegetables, lemons, nuts and fruit, strings of garlic bulbs, olive oil and wine which may be a temptation to the home cook on the eve of departure. Discriminating shopping is better done in small shops rather than the various souvenir palaces along the popular routes. Sad to say, even though many of these complexes are linked with a particular local industry and its specialist factory, very often they carry standardised goods, not all of which are made in the district, and some of which have even been imported from Spain. However, this does not always affect their interest or value, though it is greater fun, when possible, to make purchases at source after seeing some part of the process by which they are made. Leather work—handbags, gloves, footwear, luggage, wallets, spectacle cases as well as coloured suede jackets and similar clothing, are to be found in the stores attached to the tanneries of Inca, and also at the Fabrica Alvida in Santa Maria, closer to Palma. This factory will make clothing to measure. Shoes are made at Lluchmayor, Binisalem and Lloseta.

Manacor is famous for its artificial pearls, and a visit to one of the two large factories there includes a tour of the production line, where handworkers fashion very beautiful pearly globules—created by what is said to be a secret process—into both plain and intricate articles for personal ornamentation. Then there is beautiful glass from Campanet, not far from Pollensa. The highly-skilled techniques of making fine glass can be traced back to the third century under the rule of the Carthaginians, and were revived by a member of the Gordiola family in the eighteenth century.

Articles made of olive wood are on sale all over the island. Many of these are mass-produced and machine-turned, and though this does not detract from the beautiful grain of the wood, many people prefer to search for the hand-made bowls and platters of irregular shape, some very thin. Preferably, this wood should be oiled and not polished, and the process can be continued when it is put into use at home. Attractive enamelware such as boxes, ashtrays and costume jewellery are specialities of Felanitx. There is also lace-making and embroidery, handicrafts special to women of the mountain villages, whose fine work may be bought from roadside stalls at such popular places as Valldemossa. Though pharmaceutical jars, with antique lettering and decoration are another speciality, these may or may not be genuinely Majorcan. They are usually white with the Latin inscriptions in blue, and although the real thing can be seen in the apothecary's shop at the monastery of Valldemossa genuine antiques for sale are becoming increasingly rare. As in the case of these jars, plates and other decorative pottery will often turn out to have been imported from Valencia, or perhaps copied from the ware of that province. Earthenware pots are very cheap.

The best examples of these crafts may be found in the specialist shops of Palma, where there are a great many pedestrian alleys within a small radius of the important boulevards. Particular attractions include guitars at all prices made by a craftsman on the Avenida Antonio Maura, and Swiss watches and clocks which may be bought comparatively cheaply because they are tax free, though of course they are subject to taxation on importation to Britain. Beware of the occasional pedlar who may accost you on the beaches; his goods are apt to be worthless, however cheap. If interested, one should go to an established shop such as the watchmaker who has been in business for nearly a century in the Calle Colon, near the Ayuntamiento. Inlaid furniture is another Majorcan speciality, probably too bulky to carry home, though it is possible to make arrangements for such things to be shipped abroad. Old maps and prints based on the work of Majorca's famous cartographers can be discovered in various shops; reproductions coming at attractive prices. But perhaps most diverting of all is the *Rastro* or Saturday morning 'flea market' which spills over a stretch of the easterly segment of Palma's encircling avenue. As distinct from ordinary shopping, this must be an occasion for driving bargains, or attempting to do so. Meanwhile the less adventurous of the family can always while away their time under the familiar protective umbrella of Woolworth's at the meeting point of the Avenida Rey Jaime III and the Paseo Generalissimo Franco, two of the main thoroughfares of the city.

2 Palma de Mallorca

Happy those people who in earlier days came to Palma by sea, to be greeted by its fairytale cathedral with its tiers of pinnacles, golden even when the sun is not shining. For the majority of present-day travellers who arrive by air, with probably a final coach journey to the resort of their choice, I recommend that they make their way, within a day or two, to the island's capital, and especially to the seafront, in the meantime closing their eyes to the other distractions of a city which combines lively modernity with the dignity of other centuries.

Palma was originally a walled city, and this has had a constricting effect upon the siting of its medieval monuments, making streets in its old quarter narrow and rambling, and setting churches, palaces and civic buildings so close together that sometimes it is impossible to get a clear view of their exteriors. The walls originally enclosed a small area, but after the conquest of the island by the Moors they were extended. The last phase of their rebuilding was completed in 1116 and, subject to various restoration work, they endured into the nineteenth century, after which they were almost totally demolished to make way for a broad ring road. A glance at the map shows that this boulevard consists of angles which define the site of the battlements, of which hardly anything remains in any part of the city. The seaward dèfences too, have gone by the board in a major land reclamation scheme aimed both at protecting the city from flooding as well as extending the port area and providing an imposing motor route along the south and seaward edge of the city, below some of its finest buildings. Coming in from the east, the Ronda Litoral passes the Cathedral and the galleried Almudaina Palace and its gardens, then becomes the Paseo Sagrera which gives access to the famous Lonja or medieval Stock Exchange, and the neighbouring Consulado del Mar or Admiralty Court—both buildings of prime importance in the days of Palma's commercial glory—before continuing as the Paseo Maritimo below the antique windmills of Es Jonquet and finally becoming one of the principal highways linking the holiday resorts on that side of the city.

Other structural changes have affected medieval Palma. At one point it was divided in two by a seasonal torrent, La Riera, which though dry in summer at other times was subject to disastrous flooding, turning it into a torrent worthy of the name, causing grievous loss in terms of life and property. In the autumn of 1403 alone it drowned more than 5000 citizens. At last, but not until 1623, the course of the river was diverted to the east, forcing it to keep to the channel of what had been the city moat. The natural riverbed is now transformed into two spacious shopping streets: Rambla or Via Roma where flower sellers add colour to its central island, and the Paseo Generalissimo Franco, otherwise known as El Borne, which not only is the most popular promenade for Palma's citizens in their ritual evening walkabout or *paseo,* but also makes one of the most logical starting points for major sightseeing expeditions, beginning from its seaward end.

Physically and chronologically one might as well start with the Almudaina Palace, the ancient residence of the Moorish Walis or Governors. Not only has it a splendid position overlooking the Bay of Palma, but also its capture by King Jaime I and his nobles opens one of the most interesting phases in the life of the city, and of the whole island group. However, though the architectural theme of the palace is Moorish, as instanced by the arcaded windows looking out to sea, the whole complex was almost totally rebuilt for use by the new kings not only as a fortress but as a splendid residence. The Moorish remains are few, and the most notable of these are the arch in the gardens of S'Hort del Rey to the west and the ornamental pool set into the walls bounding the Ronda or open space, which was for traditional defensive reasons left unoccupied. It could be that this wide arch once formed a means of access to the palace by water, for the convenience of the Walis in the days when the sea came up to the palace walls. Nowadays the entrance to this beautiful building is from its east side, near the head of a flight of steps commanded by a plain wooden cross, and immediately opposite the west façade of the Cathedral, which crowds in upon its sister building, separated only by a pavement.

An archway leads into the huge courtyard of the Almudaina Palace, beyond an office where tickets are issued. Look up at the decorated ceiling of the arch on the way through. From this point onwards this dignified building around its spacious quadrangle is entirely evocative of Majorca's own kings, despite its Moorish overtones. Jaime II spent the last 12 years of his life here, furnishing the palace with such luxuries as a roof garden, a menagerie and an elaborate plumbing system. Much of the work of conversion was assigned to Pedro Selva, who is equally renowned as the architect of the Castle of Bellver, which guards the western sea approaches. Selva was assisted by one Francisco Campredon, a native of Perpignan, a specialist in metal work who is believed to have created the angel which surmounts the palace's central tower.

A series of formal and lofty state rooms, all on the ground floor, have been set aside for public viewing. Tours are conducted by multi-lingual guides, and there is no scope for individual sightseeing. This is partly because a very large part of the palace, which is traditionally arranged round the four sides of its inner courtyard, is forbidden territory, since it houses not only the headquarters of the Captain General of the Balearic Islands and the provincial Courts of Justice and Archives, but even more sacrosanctly, contains on its upper floor and within those arcades which look so beguiling from outside, a whole range of rooms set aside as the official residence of the Spanish Head of State if and when he visits the capital of his island province.

Those state apartments open to the public are on the south side of the courtyard. What was originally a huge vaulted reception hall is divided into three large communicating rooms, including a throne room, all of which are furnished with Spanish and Flemish tapestries and furniture. The portraits of the Majorcan kings, and various historic tableaux, though not of enormous artistic merit, form a graphic exposition of history, as for instance the one showing the victorious Christian fleet entering Corfu after the defeat of the Turks at the battle of Lepanto in 1571. Also within the historical context there is a beautifully designed family tree setting out the lineage of the Kings of Spain. The King's Apartments, which lead one from another, are furnished with taste and without clutter. Those once occupied by the Queen are now set aside for the Captain General's use.

The conducted tour usually ends with a visit to the small chapel of Santa Aña, on the west side of the courtyard, through an attractive Romanesque arch. Yet the single nave of the church with its arched roof is pure Gothic. This may come as a reminder of the antecedents of the first kings of Majorca, since this little chapel of theirs is similar in design to that of the Holy Cross attached to the royal palace of Perpignan. Features of special interest include the painted reredos behind the main altar, with its side panels depicting St George and St Vidal. The remains of St Praxedes in a side chapel are objects of special veneration, as he was a local man martyred during the persecution of the Christian Mozarabs in the last stages of Moslem oppression.

After the fall of the kingdom of Majorca and its return to mainland dominance, Pedro IV of Aragon decreed that the Almudaina should be demoted to use as a prison. Part was subsequently allotted for use by an alchemist, so as to facilitate his researches into the practicalities of converting base metals into gold—an understandably obsessive medieval aspiration, and one which is only minimally nearer achievement in the atomic age. Otherwise this beautiful and dignified building was used on isolated occasions by later Spanish monarchs.

One moves into another world by crossing the pavement which separates the Almudaina Palace from the Cathedral, though it is in the styles of architecture rather than the period of their building that they differ so greatly. The great Gothic cathedral, or La Seo as it is affectionately known in the Majorcan dialect, is an arresting sight both by reason of its elaborate Gothic architecture and the mellow stone, quarried near Santañy to the east of the island, of which it is built. The one disappointment is that its proximity to the palace prevents the full glory of its western façade receiving all the attention it deserves. This congestion of the site is explained by the fact that Palma was originally walled to a more limited extent than that defined by the later medieval fortifications, and when the cathedral was projected there was no available space for the grassy quadrangles, courtyards, splashing fountains and wide perspectives allowed by the conventional parvis of continental cathedrals.

Though Palma's cathedral was many years, even centuries, in the building, it was conceived in an emergency. When Jaime I was poised to make his historic landing it seemed more than likely that his enterprise would be defeated by storms. Accordingly he vowed that in return for divine protection he would raise a lasting monument in stone and dedicate it to the Blessed Virgin. As it happens, at the time of his death in 1276 the only part of the building to be completed was the Chapel of the Holy Trinity, which now occupies the apse at the east end. Three and a half centuries were to elapse before the last of many stages was reached, with the employment of scores of master craftsmen and considerable financial assistance from Majorcan nobles who in recompense had their coats of arms incorporated into the vaulted roof of the interior. The High

Altar was consecrated in 1327, but it was not until the early
seventeenth century that the west front with its great carved
doorway was completed. Subsequently the cathedral remained
externally unchanged, except for repairs and shoring-up
operations to the west front.

But first to get one long view of the cathedral, such as was
the reassuring experience of Palma's medieval merchant
seamen. As seen from the harbour there is nothing austere
about the building—far from it. Its geometry is based on
massive buttresses soaring to pinnacles, and above these are
flying buttresses, again with tiers of turrets aligned with the
roof, and all studded with the decorative knobs which are a
feature of Gothic architecture. Very few windows are apparent
from the south side, because most of the spaces where they
might have been are blocked with masonry, and other higher
ones are invisible from ground level. The most interesting
feature is the great south door, set slightly left of centre. This
entrance to the cathedral, known as the Mirador because of its
position as a viewpoint from which to survey the harbour and
the bay beyond, incorporates many beautiful sculptures of
combined Majorcan and foreign craftsmanship. The tympanum or arched space above the double doors depicts the Last
Supper, while the decoration of the arches is typically Flemish.
The five statues standing in niches, representing biblical
figures, were intended to have 52 companions, but these were
never installed. A central Madonna and Child in Carrara
marble has had to be removed to the nearby Diocesan Museum
because it was weathering badly.

Because this entrance to the cathedral is kept closed, the
thing to do now is to make one's back to the west façade and its
imposing entrance, to compare the late sixteenth century
carvings with those of the earlier door, even at the risk of a
crick in the neck. This time the splendid tympanum depicts the
Virgin Mary in her role as patroness. She is accompanied by
sun and moon and palm trees, which have come to be regarded
as the island's emblems. The two balancing towers, rising to a
height of 63 metres, were added to strengthen the structure
after earthquake damage in the nineteenth century. Unfortunately these 'mock Gothic' additions have obscured two rose
windows which the original designers had intended should
balance those at the east end of the cathedral. However, the
portal and the central rose window are genuine sixteenth
century.

As this great west entrance is opened on ceremonial
occasions only, another right-angled turn must be made along

the northern flank of the building. Beyond the Almoina (or Alms) Door which was built in 1498, we see the belfry, which departs from the Gothic style in its rectangular plainness, deriving from the Catalan style of architecture. The pride of this tower is the largest of its nine bells, known as N'Eloi, which was cast in 1389: Its weight is so great that it takes 12 men to ring it, while its reverberations have been known to shatter stained glass in the cathedral.

But now the time has come to go inside, rather inappropriately through pay turnstiles, and directed through the Treasury, where vestments, ancient music manuscripts, jewelled crucifixes, silver candelabra, paintings and many other beautiful things are exhibited. But first things first. To make up for the restriction and delay of being unable to enter the cathedral through any one of its important doors, this must be a time for skipping detailed examination of treasures in favour of a clear sight of the interior. And this is a breath-taking experience in its revelation of airiness, light and simplicity—so very much in contrast to the intricate decoration of the exterior.

When the overall impression has sunk in, anyone would be forgiven for wondering how it can possibly be that 14 columns can be so tall and so slender, and yet carry the weight of such a gigantic span of roof. They have in fact been compared, time and time again, to palm trees, because of the manner in which they branch out, as into fronds, at a height of over 21 metres. It is at this moment that the more logical among us, who have done their reconnaissance well, will remember the massive external buttresses, which in fact bear a large proportion of the load. Their presence also accounts for 14 side chapels set into the spaces between the masonry of the north and south outer walls. But these too can be ignored for the moment, despite the lure of their pictures and baroque furnishings, and even though one of them contains (for our insular interest) a painting which includes the Duke of Wellingtom, as it were 'snapped' when supporting a noble friend on the field of battle during the Peninsular War.

The best vantage point for viewing churches and cathedrals is always their west end. Standing here, with our backs to the closed Great Door, we see that there are three naves, all of the same length, though the central one continues unobstructed by rood screen or intervening choir stalls into the further Royal Chapel, which would otherwise be a church in itself. For this length of vision we may thank one Antonio Gaudi, a specialist in Catalan/Gothic architecture, who was commissioned after the turn of the present century to restore the interior of the cathedral to an approximation of its original appearance. His principal operation was to open up the chancel around and beyond the High Altar. The effect is enhanced, rather surprisingly, by the provision of a contorted Art Nouveau canopy over the altar. This reflects Gaudi's personal taste, and incidentally has turned full circle to win popular approval. The feeling of spaciousness provided by Gaudi is of course based on the cathedral's beautifully graceful columns, which in fact are second in height only to those of the Duomo in Milan, while being only half their diameter. Chartres and Rheims, and our own English cathedrals, come nowhere in this architectural contest. Light is provided by all 32 of the windows, the most important of which is the gigantic rose window in the central apse. This is claimed to be the largest in the world, being 12.5 metres in diameter. It is said to contain 1236 pieces of coloured glass, which to me are reminiscent of the prisms of a giant snowflake. A smaller rose window lights the apse of the central chapel, at a lower level, and two more are set in the apses of the lateral naves, as well as another large one above the Great Door. Tall lights in the intervals between the outer buttresses, and therefore high up, depict scenes from the Book of Daniel, while some relate to the Messianic prophecies. The filling-in of others was done by way of reinforcement.

We reach the Chapel Royal beyond the ancient High Altar, passing also two baroque lecterns, one for the reading of the Gospel, and the other for the Epistle. The vaulted roof of the chapel is lower. Among the most important details here must be the 110 choir stalls fashioned by Camprédon in 1328 from walnut, and carved in the form of animals. With history in mind, it is a matter for regret that King Jaime I, who after all was responsible for this chapel which during his lifetime was to take the place of a mosque after it had been ritually purified, is buried in relative obscurity at Poblet in Spain, together with many of his Aragonese kinsmen. Nevertheless, the remains of the next two Majorcan sovereigns, Jaime II and III, repose in niches in the wall dividing the Royal Chapel from its continuation, the Chapel of the Holy Trinity.

Even in a limited area sightseeing is an exhausting business, so that after the necessary return through the Treasury, and perhaps a diversion into the cloister—where incidentally there is a well-kept lavatory—it may be as well to postpone visiting the Diocesan Museum in the ancient Episcopal Palace, which is only a short distance beyond the east end of the cathedral on its seaward side. But with time in hand this is a cool place to linger, and there are many lovely things to see, including early paintings, rare books and manuscripts, baroque altar screens, and other church furnishings. Another attraction is the close view of the harbour from a gallery above what was once part of the sea walls—a sight which is rendered doubly fascinating by comparison with a splendid picture of St George and the Dragon against a background of that very same harbour complete with a mass of shipping.

The Episcopal Palace is on the edge of one of the oldest quarters of the town, known as the Portella, where the paved streets are lined with solid stone-built houses in earth colours. Their carved, overhanging eaves below tiled roofs throw the narrow streets into deep shadow, which makes it difficult to judge the angle of the sun, and consequently in which direction one may be wandering. Traffic is one-way, and pedestrians dive into doorways to allow it to pass. Though the vaguely Italianate architecture owes a great deal to the Renaissance, in some respects these streets are unlike their counterparts in the northern Mediterranean; there is no washing strung across from one house to another, nor bright splashes of colour, nor much evidence as to the day to day life of the citizens. The explanation is that the houses are entered through massive archways which open into courtyards which once contained stables and domestic offices, while the life of the household proper began, rather remotely, on the first floor or *piso principal*, which is reached by a grand staircase, very often dividing into two and opening on to an upper gallery. In observing the style of these grand and sturdy buildings, some of which may be visited, others of which the courtyard only is accessible, one must remember that a disastrous fire destroyed whole streets in the sixteenth century, after which the medieval Gothic buildings were replaced in the Italian idiom, in which, incidentally, rectangular windows with grilles were substituted for the previous Gothic *azimez* or twin-lighted ones with pointed tops. The new fashion introduced not only classic columns and statuary, but also carved medallions and other decoration, very often of fruit and flowers, in the more florid Plateresque style. It was in this great rebuilding period, between 1650 and 1750, that the doorways were enlarged to admit coaches, their heavily carved wooden doors being cleverly balanced on pivots, in the Moorish manner.

This profusion of great, secretive houses, each bearing the name of some important Majorcan family, are worthy of their rank as palaces. They evidence Palma's period of commercial interchange with other Mediterranean countries and city states.

The merchant princes lived well, if formally, in large inter-communicating saloons, the walls of which were usually panelled in red pine and hung with priceless tapestries. Furniture was carved and upholstered in leather or velvet, while painted wooden coffers housed the family possessions. It was not unusual for an altar screen to be included in the bedroom furniture.

There are a great many of these palaces in Palma. They have their counterparts in country houses—most of them within a easy ride or drive of the city—which also have been given the name of the family owning them, prefixed by the word *Son,* which may be translated as the French 'chez' or 'belonging to.' Among the town houses particular mention should be made of the Vivot Palace, in the Calle Zavella, east of the church of St Eulalia. This has a deceptively plain exterior and a courtyard of splendid arches supported by pillars of ruddy marble, and the usual grand staircase leading to a gallery overlooking the patio. Then there is the sixteenth-century Olezo Palace in the Calle Morey, and the earlier Casa Oleo in the Calle Almudaina, where sculptures, ceramics and ancient coinage are on display. One of the most impressive exteriors is that of the Casa Marqués de Palmer, in the Calle del Sol.

Two of the few surviving Arab remains are to be found in the Portella quarter. First, at No 13 Calle de Serra, there are Arab baths, a miniature form of the underwater cisterns of Constantinople. (These baths are usually kept locked, but their guardian may be contacted at No. 11 Calle Portella, the parallel street.) The 12 columns which support horseshoe-shaped arches are thought to have been brought from a Roman site. Further on there is the Almudaina Arch, the sole survivor of five gates to the Saracen citadel.

If one passes under this arch, walking north-west, and then turns right for a short distance into the Avenue General Goded, one comes upon the small but open Plaza Cort, on the edge of the shopping district. This square is dominated by the beautiful Renaissance three-storeyed Ayuntamiento or Town Hall, with its deep, carved eaves overhanging one of the most beautiful civic buildings of the seventeenth century. The bell in its clock tower, known as En Figuera, once served as a warning of invasion, and latterly of fire. Two entrances lead to a covered courtyard. Between these there are seats reserved for old age pensioners—a happy idea—and above them a balustraded window from which civic dignitaries may watch processions and ceremonial occasions. The interior of the building has suffered rather from its rebuilding in 1894 after a fire, but for those who are interested the attached municipal Library and Museum are worth visiting. The latter contains not only a wealth of illuminated manuscripts covering royal decrees from as early as the thirteenth century, but a series of portraits—not all of them of artistic merit but chosen for historical reasons, as is the policy of London's National Portrait Gallery—depicting famous Majorcans, and people associated with the island's story. The range is wide, though some of the likenesses must be open to doubt, as for instance the picture of Hannibal, the great Carthaginian, and Saint Sebastian, as well as rulers, lawmakers and churchmen.

There is a smaller piazza tucked away behind the Ayuntamiento, one which is fairly quiet, and has café tables set out on a shady pavement. The dominant feature is the church of Santa Eulalia, set on a site less crowded than many another city church. The entrance and tower happen to be comparatively new, if judged against the main body of the church. But great unity is found in the interior, due not only to the architect's concept, based upon the spanning of the aisles by a single roof, but also because, most unusually, it was built within the course of 25 years only, a very short space of time for a building of such importance. But this was immediately after the reconquest, when zeal ran high. Many important events have taken place in the church of Santa Eulalia, from periods as far back as gatherings in the reign of Jaime II, and the later mass conversion of the Jewish citizenry in 1435, as well as one of the final chapters of a *cause célèbre* concerning Ramon Llull's love affair with a married woman. But the story of this holy man belongs more to the church of San Francisco, which is only a few minutes walk away.

Of all Palma's proliferation of churches, the conventual church of San Francisco must be the most beautiful and important, and can be recommended even to visitors who are not particularly interested in such sights. Great churches, many of them Gothic as to exterior and baroque in their interior decoration and furnishings, are encountered with little warning during any exploration of the old city. The conventual church of Santa Margarita, near the end of the Calle de San-Miguel, rescued from use as a warehouse and now a National Monument is one such. Another is the nearby church of San Miguel, on the site of a mosque where mass was celebrated immediately after the reconquest; it is not itself very old, but enshrines the miraculous image of the Virgin of Health, which accompanied Jaime I aboard ship. Montesión in the *calle* of that name which now houses a Jesuit school, and is notable for its baroque entrance; the Church of the Sacred Cross, fifteenth and sixteenth-century Gothic, with a crypt under its High Altar—there are many more. Generally they possess a single nave which without loss of height ends in an apse at the east end. As we travel the island later on, we will see that country churches are different, being usually rectangular and built in a combination of earth and stone, and with timber roofs, which explains why they have not lasted as well as their city counterparts. Most of Palma's are in fact of the style known as Catalan-Gothic, buttressed and with side chapels. Though many were built immediately after the reconquest, their interior decoration is usually of a later date and owes its distinction to the work of Italian craftsmen. Much of this embellishment was delayed until after the completion of work inside the Cathedral, which naturally took precedence.

To return to the Church of San Francisco. This dates from 1281, when Jaime II laid its foundation stone in commemoration of his eldest son's renunciation of the succession in favour of a monastic life. The first mass was celebrated here in 1317. The best of the Baroque of the interior—and there is a great deal of it—is the work of Francisco Herrera, who had learned his skills in Rome before being brought to Majorca in 1690 to work explicitly on redecorating the Cathedral and contemporary Gothic churches. He is responsible for the lovely west façade, as well as for the central altar with its golden pillars and latticed galleries designed to accommodate the choir. Of the five side chapels in the apse, the first on the north side contains the effigy of Ramon Llull. His late Gothic tomb incorporates a set of niches which were originally intended to contain allegorical figures representing his diverse interests: grammar and logic, geometry and arithmetic, astrology, music, rhetoric and foreign languages.

This great man was born to a noble family in Palma about 1235. His early life was profligate, exemplified by his passion for the wife of a Palma merchant, whom he pursued to the point of exhibitionism by riding his horse up the steps into the body of the Church of Santa Eulalia when the lady was at her devotions. Goaded and shocked to the extreme, in order to convince him of the error of his ways, this virtuous woman invited him ostensibly to an amorous meeting, when to his horror she exposed her breasts, revealing them to be eaten by cancerous growths. The effect was shattering. Ramon Llull immediately went into religious retreat, then embarked on extensive travels, writing and teaching as he went. In all he is responsible for more than 200 books on erudite subjects, written in Latin, Catalan and even Arabic. Upon his return to his native land he set up a school of Arabic studies on the north-west coast of the island, but later, not being content to commit himself to a sedentary life, he set off again to convert the Moslems of North Africa to Christianity. Reputedly he died a martyr's death in Algeria, and has been beatified by the Roman Catholic church, often a first step towards canonization.

The famous cloisters belonging to the Franciscan monastery to which Ramon Llull was attached, are reached through doors on the south side of the church, after paying a small fee for the privilege. Dalliance in these restful surroundings would be worthwhile at any price. The paved walk is shaded by columns supporting a painted roof, and an upper tier of arches forms a gallery around the quadrangle, while a higher storey still incorporates the friars' dormitory and cells. Lawns, palm trees, flowering shrubs and a central well almost complete the picture, but there is one final touch: the belfry which rises, like a minaret, above the nave of the church. A school presently occupies one side of the cloisters, and therefore is out of bounds to visitors, but the Treasury, which is an integral part of the design of the church, now houses an interesting collection of religious objects, including manuscripts and paintings, following its use as a prison in the nineteenth century.

In common with others possessing a long and varied history, Palma is a city of contrasts. One can step immediately from monastic peace and seclusion into a metropolitan scene, bustling with people. With experience the stranger to the town will soon discover some central point of orientation, such as the Plaza Mayor, which, incidentally, has a large underground car park. This spacious paved square, closed to traffic, has shopping streets radiating in all directions—those to the west being reached by descending staircases adjoining the Teatro Principal, which has recently been restored. This is the direction from which we reach the Via Roma, otherwise La Rambla; and, by the Paseo de General Mola, the Avenida Rey Jaime III, an important arcaded main street of good shops, banks and offices which include, usefully, the bureau of the National Tourist Office. Another rewarding direction to take is towards the more commercial part of the city, through a narrow opening in one of the longer sides of the rectangular 'square' of the plaza. This leads into the Calle de San Miguel which heads straight past—on the left—San Miguel's Church and—on the right—the Church of San Antonio, at the rear of which there is a most intriguing covered market, which is to be recommended to all visitors who relish displays of country produce. It is almost exclusively a food market, open every day, and thronged by housewives who in the continental manner do their shopping in small quantities, one day at a time. For even more colourful activity, the visitor is advised to make a point of visiting Palma's 'Flea Market' or *Rastro,* Saturday mornings only, in the avenues between the Plaza San Antonio and the sea. Here are to be found the usual fascinating jumble of old clothes, spare parts, bric-a-brac and trifles of indeterminate use which can occupy treasure seekers for hours on end. Incidentally, here and here only people are advised to bargain when buying. Elsewhere one would be apt to run into trouble, or at any rate commit a breach of good manners.

Immediately north of the Plaza Olivar and the covered market we reach the Plaza d'España, the point of arrival and departure for the local bus services from the eastern suburbs and coast resorts, notably Arenal. The two railway stations are here, next to each other, the smaller one serving the gay, but at the same time practical, service to Soller and intervening mountain villages.

At this point in our wanderings it might be as well to haul ourselves back into the present century and to realise the changes which have taken place in Palma within a very short period, in terms of its history. Electricity was brought to the city in 1902, and in that year the first luxury hotel was opened. Communications were speeded up with the introduction of a reliable steamer service between Palma and Barcelona. In the following decade, when most of Europe was at war, electric tramways were built to link the suburbs with the city centre. These have now been replaced by frequent bus services. Then, to keep pace with the rapid growth of the tourist industry and the influx of seasonal visitors in the 1950s and 1960s, major reconstruction of the town was undertaken. This consisted principally of the opening up of boulevards and other luxury shopping streets, and the creation of gardens in whatever open spaces could be found. Of these, the s'Hort del Rey, below the Almudaina walls, are perhaps the most relaxing. At the same time the interest of commercial growth ran parallel, and involved the construction of an outer port and the inauguration of a modernised airport to the east of the city. This now caters for one of the heaviest loads of air-borne travellers in Europe. It was about this time, too, that the coastal road was extended and widened to cope with the mushroom growths of tourist developments both to the east and west of the city.

The sea is the key to the city, and to the island's history. And the easiest way of reaching it is down El Borne, which splits the town in two. Any deviation to the westward from the modern boulevard will reveal more narrow streets on the medieval pattern, some with their quota of ancient town houses. One of the most typical and charming is the Morell Palace, in the Calle Cateyano, which has an exceptionally well proportioned double staircase leading up from its courtyard. Another is the Montenegro Palace, nearby in the calle of that name.

About 100 yards before it would reach the sea front, El Borne becomes the Avenida Antonio Maura. This is a place for watching life go by, without stress or aching feet. Fascinating sights present themselves in the bay of Palma and ashore which can be enjoyed either from a seat in a quayside café or fish restaurant, or from under the palms of the Paseo Sagrera. The shore, with its distinct areas for merchant shipping and for yachts and smaller craft curves in a south-westerly direction, with a fast motor road which links the city's westerly resorts, each with its complement of high-rise hotels and apartments blocks. Backing them closely are the foothills and high mountains which contribute grandeur to the scene. It was not many miles along this coast that King Jaime I made his historic landing and advanced to storm the walls of what was then a Moorish stronghold. Those walls have since been flattened and lie beneath the promenade, which continues as far as the outlet of the Torrente La Riera, whose seasonal flow now is channeled harmlessly west of the town. The Almudaina Palace and the Cathedral, now behind us, are reminders of the glorious epoch of history in which the Majorcan dynasty was established. Another reminder of this period comes with the sight of Bellver Castle, in its commanding position to the west, overlooking the whole city and its approaches.

Bellver was built by Jaime II to be not only a watchtower and defence, but also to function as, say, Windsor Castle in relation to Buckingham Palace. Nevertheless, as well as its virtues as a royal residence, it is considered to be one of the finest military buildings of the fourteenth century. Built of yellow sandstone, it was begun as early as 1309. The design is circular, with all its rooms built around a great central courtyard open to the sky. At opposite quarters there are three towers, while a fourth is joined to the main structure by a bridge at high level spanning what was a moat. This tower was the quarters of the military garrison, situated conveniently above the dungeons. The castle is unique in the separation of its residential quarters from the military—a plan which allows for a degree of elegance in the architectural design of the circular structure. At ground level there is a complete circle of rounded Romanesque arches facing inward. These are surmounted, without visual conflict, by another complete series of arches, this time pointed and Gothic, above which there is a promenade within the ramparts.

The history of Bellver is not all glory. Though King Sancho spent some time there in 1314, even before it was completed, little further use was made of it as a royal residence. Otherwise it was periodically inhabited as a refuge against revolt and, another enemy, the plague. Then in the sixteenth century common criminals were imprisoned in it, and it was later to function as a prison for French officers during the Napoleonic Wars. The dungeons still bear witness of the scribbled initials and names of some of these unhappy men. Nowadays Bellver belongs to the city of Palma, and is open to the public, and houses a small but interesting museum. It should be put well to the forefront of sight-seeing plans, not only for its own merits, but because it constitutes the best viewpoint of Palma and all the country which lies around it. It is about two miles from the main city, and about the same distance from the coast, and is approached by a steep road rising to 140 metres by hairpin bends, so that a car or taxi is the easiest way up, whereas the descent is easier, down stony paths through the pinewoods.

But perhaps this expedition can wait while one takes a breather at sea level. In the immediate foreground, facing the Paseo Sagrera, there are two lovely and important historic buildings which testify to the period of commercial prosperity which resulted from the Christian reconquest of the island and which lasted some hundreds of years until, in fact, it was unforeseeably ended by the discovery of the Americas, which completely altered the trading patterns of Spain and the countries of the western Mediterranean. Majorca was then relegated to comparative obscurity. But in the meantime a magnificent Stock Exchange had been built, with the idea not only of coping efficiently with the flux of goods arriving and departing by sea immediately beneath the city walls, but also of vying in splendour with similar buildings enjoyed by Majorca's competitors, the city states of the Mediterranean.

The Lonja, as it is called, fulfilled both these aspirations, as a functional mercantile exchange where business was transacted, and as one of the most beautiful 'all-of-one-piece' medieval buildings in Palma. It is built of Santañy granite, in the style known as Gothic civic, and its design was entrusted in 1426 to a Majorcan architect by the name of Guillermo Sagrera, who was also responsible for much of what is best in the Cathedral and Episcopal Palace. Observers may notice points of resemblance

between the Lonja's entrance, from a small square east of the
building, and the Cathedral's Almoina portal, which in point of
fact was designed in 1498 by Francisco Sagrera, Guillermo's
son. There were insufferable delays in building, when the
Palma merchants who had commissioned the project defaulted
and failed to pay Guillermo's fees. Far from being finished in
15 years, as had been estimated, the work hung fire until in
desperation the architect, having been driven to sue for his
money, left for Naples in order to undertake more lucrative
work for King Alfonso V of Aragon. His place on the Lonja
site was then taken by his brother, Miguel, to whom is
attributed a great deal of the sculpture included in the overall
design, which is strangely ecclesiastical while still being
purpose-built for commerce. The interior consists of a single
spacious chamber, lighted by pointed glazed Gothic windows,
making one large open rectangular floor interrupted only by a
double row of six columns, twisted into barley-sugar Solomonic
curves, and branching out gracefully to support the vaulted
roof. The octagonal turrets at each corner of the building
originally housed spiral staircases leading to the roof, from
which there is a superb view, one which would have been of
particular interest when the merchants using the Lonja were
intimately concerned with the comings and goings of ships, and
those moored at its very walls. This of course was in the days
before the land to seaward had been reclaimed. The arch at the
edge of the gardens, which has been moved from its original
site, was once the entrance to the city from the port area. When
the island's trade went into decline, the Lonja came to be
disregarded, and eventually fell into use as a common
storehouse for agricultural produce. Happily it has since been
rescued, and is now open to the public as the Provincial Fine
Arts Museum, which houses art exhibitions of typically Majorcan significance.

The next building of importance, to the west of the arch, is
later in period. The Consueldo del Mar, or Admiralty Court,
was built in the seventeenth century. The upper of its two
storeys incorporates a beautiful Renaissance gallery of five
arches with a decorative painted ceiling, overlooking the sea.
The small Oratory behind the building has a typically Gothic
façade. The Consueldo del Mar Museum, which occupies the
main building, contains such things as charts, naval instruments, portraits and model ships.

However much or little culture and sight-seeing visitors to
Palma may wish to absorb at one time, they are unlikely to wish
to turn their backs upon the modern entertainment provided

for them. Bull-fighting aside, there is one whole district of the city, slightly off centre, which caters for rather extrovert night, and even daytime life. To reach this, one crosses La Riera in the direction of Bellver Castle. By bearing inland opposite the yacht harbour and behind the windmills of Es Jonquet, one gets soon to El Pueblo Espanol, which is a custom-built Spanish village, complete with reproductions of certain aspects of Spanish architecture, including town walls, entrance gates and reproductions of famous Spanish monuments. Within the compass of a few steps, then, the tourist is invited to visit the Alhambra in Granada, Toledo, and the Golden Tower of Seville, or otherwise to make his choice of restaurants, workshops, stalls and a folk theatre and nightclub where the island dances, and also flamenco, are performed. Apart from this concentration of entertainment, but not far away, we reach the outlying district of Palma known as El Terreno, where restaurants, night clubs and discotheques are centred around the Plaza Gomila, and have a more authentic atmosphere.

3 Palma's Beaches

A capital city is seldom the ideal place for relaxation, even when its central hotels are equipped with swimming pools and every other luxury. A lengthy catalogue of history revealed round every corner, combined with other people's hurry and busy traffic is inclined to undermine the lotus eater's morale. So it has to be recognised that the majority of northern visitors give way to a compulsive urge towards sun, sea, sand and scenery. When it became evident that tourism must become a major industry in Majorca, Palma was quick to realise its natural advantages. The beaches on either side of the city were not only eminently suitable for development, but they were also varied enough to attract a wide range of tourists drawn from many foreign countries and, what is more, with differing tastes and in various income brackets. Good links by road was one key to schemes which were to extend Palma into one long chain of seaside resorts, all within easy reach of the city itself. This works both ways, of course, so that the nearest beaches are popular with Palma's inhabitants, and tend to become crowded. It follows that visitors who prefer an away-from-it-all holiday should look further afield, and to other coasts—in fact to the north, east and west of the island.

It is noticeable upon leaving Palma by the Paseo Maritimo in a south-westerly direction that the holiday atmosphere immediately takes over, even though Majorca's history nudges one from time to time in the form of topographical reminders that it was from this direction that King Jaime I made the landing in the autumn of 1229 which was to lead to his speedy reconquest of the island. The highway follows the curve of the Bay of Palma, except where rocky spurs of land jut out into the sea. These pine-clad extensions of the foothills of the mountain chain have the effect of dividing this part of the coast into sections, each containing its own resort, and usually with sandy beaches enfolded by rocks. Each beach is apt to have its own individuality and its own adherents.

To begin the journey, whether by car, coach or bus service,

the Paseo Maritimo bypasses the archaic and now well-preserved survivors of the windmills of Es Jonquet in the old Santa Catalina district. This fast road is open on its seaward side, and the entire sweep of the bay, with its shipping and mercantile life remains in view, while the landward side is flanked by a succession of tall hotels and apartment blocks built over shops and places of entertainment, comprising the Terreno developments. Bellver Castle on its pine-speckled hill overlooks the deep-water port, where transatlantic and cruise-ships berth, and asserts its connection with the fifteenth century Tower of Pelaires, which was built at sea level in defence of Porto Pi. At one time a chain was slung between two towers, effectively closing the port, which in those early days was Palma's only harbour; nowadays it is largely given over to pleasure craft.

The string of tourist developments which contribute to Palma's popularity as a holiday region begins almost immediately with Cala Mayor. Its name, meaning 'great bay', flatters it, as in fact it possesses quite a small though admittedly sandy beach. Because this is the nearest to Palma, it is apt to become crowded in summer and at weekends. The road then winds uphill through the charming San Agustin district before descending to Ca's Catala and the urban boundary of Palma. Then once more the road is forced a short distance inland of the rocky headland of Illetas, which has its smart hotels set in steep ground studded with pines, overlooking smooth rocks where people sunbathe like seals, and a string of tiny offshore islets. Portals Nous is two kilometres further on; it has been well developed, with beautiful villas as it were pressed into the hillsides, and well masked by trees. Castillo de Bendinat is off the road to the right. This name, which when translated from the Catalan tongue reads as *bien manger* has been given to the castle because it was here that Jaime I is believed to have eaten his first meal after arriving on what was to become his kingdom, and, what is more, expressed his satisfaction with the fare provided—welcome no doubt after a stormy passage. The present castle dates from the eighteenth century.

Beyond Portals Nous, between the tenth and eleventh kilometre stone from Palma, there is a fine Dolphinarium which may be reached by sea from Palma, as well as being close to the Playa de Palma Nova in an area of development which is the most level on this side of the city. Because of the excellence of beaches hereabouts a great many people come along to enjoy them, while shady shopping boulevards cater for a thriving holiday trade.

The coast takes a distinct turn to the south at Palma Nova, in the shape of a promontory which marks the westerly limits of the bay. The highway cuts across its neck for Santa Ponsa, the scene of that unforgettable landing, and onwards to Paguera and Andraitx. All three of these places are far enough apart and self-contained enough not to be regarded as satellites of the city. This is not quite true of Magaluf, which is 2 kilometres beyond Palma Nova, though now actually joined to it by developments which follow an up-hill and down-dale pattern. Magaluf is one of the most recent of these resorts to be developed, and though it has had teething troubles it is currently well on the way to becoming one of the most extrovert along this edge of the bay.

The curious visitor would be well advised not to allow himself to become so totally preoccupied with the sea and its pleasures as to be unaware of the country lying behind the coastal strip. In this part of the island the rising ground, and the comparative dearth of buildings, except in the matter of small houses inhabited by local people and larger villas owned by some of Palma's wealthy families who built them as an escape from the heat of the sun in summer, brings a welcome change in outlook and climate. An easy expedition into the hills from Palma can be made by heading along the Calle de Andrea Doria, south of the Pueblo Español, for the village of Genova, a distance of 6 kilometres by this route, but less from Cala Mayor. Having arrived there, it is certainly worthwhile carrying on for a short distance to the Oratory of Na Burguesa, which provides a readymade platform for views of the city, the bay, and the central plain.

Then there is the rather more adventurous drive deeper into the mountains, which can be done in a circle so as to avoid using any of the passes leading to the north-west coast, which in any event is served by a dramatic corniche, an expedition which takes a greater length of time. Though a twisting mountain road leads over the Sa Creu pass in the Sierra Burguesa to join a high secondary road running parallel with the coast, an easier preliminary is to take the Bañalbufar road as far as Establiments, and from there to continue to follow the course of the Riera. Ahead now are twisting roads, not always well surfaced and promising nothing but mountain scenery, terrific distant views, and the solitude which has been banished from the shores. A road forking to the right leads through a fertile little valley to Puigpuñent, a small agricultural township, from which it is possible to continue by another minor road to the great manorial estate of Son Zafortezza with beautiful

gardens and orchards, very well watered and lush. By returning to the crossroads to the south of Puigpuñent, and to the
road from Establiments, one can continue on a somewhat
serpentine course to Galilea, another once remote village which
is worth a visit. Its plaza and church lie just to one side of the
road. From here the best view is to the north, over the tops of
pines, to the stern shape of Mount Galatzo, which at 1025
metres is one of the highest peaks in the mountain range. The
round trip may be continued by retracing one's route a short
distance, then continuing to Capdella by weaving one's way
along the flank of the mountains, before descending through
the woods to Calvia, which is about 6 kilometres from the sea at
Palma Nova.

In case any of this may seem too adventurous, a minor
excursion into the hills may be made—perhaps by taxi. In that
case the price, which has to be reckoned both in terms of
mileage and waiting time, should be agreed with the driver in
advance. This trip could go as far as Son Roca, only 7
kilometres from Palma, passing through the village of Son
Rapina which is guarded by a salient watchtower in the
grounds of a beautiful country house known as Son Cigala.
Here too is one of the best known and largest of the country
residences, Son Vidal, so typical of the elegant and sumptuous life
style of the rich families of the seventeenth and eighteenth
centuries is now a luxury hotel.

Nothing much can be said of the hinterland on the opposite
side of Palma, immediately behind the coastline. It is flat and
unproductive and only distinguished by its multitude of iron
windmills, now mostly derelict and not at all picturesque, each
with its concrete cistern which provided individual water
supplies for the smallholders in the district before piped water
was introduced. Admittedly the road leading east past the
airport goes to some fascinating places on its way to the further
coast, but it is only the narrow coastal strip which is of any
importance to some hundreds of thousands of tourists who feel
no need to look further than beach activities, coach trips, and
the shuttle service of buses plying between their resorts and the
centre of Palma.

Coming out from the city, one can diverge from the main
road leading to the airport, and instead follow the shore. For
some kilometres there are a few picturesque sights, such as the
crescent harbour of Cala Portixol, but this is too near the city to
be a hundred-per-cent healthy, and it is better to carry on for
about eight kilometres to Ca'n Pastilla by following signposts and
threading a way through streets which owe little to modernity

though less to antiquity. A sort of limbo exists until after Rabassa and the beginnings of Ca'n Pastilla, where tourism begins to take over. This resort is by no means expensive; the hotels are moderate in size, well suited for families and package tours, and the shops tend to be family-run, while at the same time there are pavement cafés, banks, night clubs, food and souvenir shops to tempt the visitor. It is from Ca'n Pastilla that one gets a first view of the main feature of this section of the coast: the Playa de Palma, which stretches for about 6 kilometres between here and Arenal, the most popular of all the resorts on this part of the coast. Hotels, cafés, apartment blocks, bars and small shops line the landward side of the road, which is served by a frequent bus service, though many people prefer the experience of travelling more expensively by horse-drawn carriage. In fact it is not far to walk, even from end to end, either along the continuous pavement bordering the sea, where there are bathing stations and various other temptations, or else to go barefoot along the sand, threading one's way between the ranks of palm-thatched umbrellas which come as a relief even to the most hardened sun-bathers.

Arenal is of recent growth. It has a little harbour, and is patronised by the masses of visitors who look for a basic though not very demanding holiday atmosphere.

4   The North-West

Without any doubt, the region lying to the north and west of Palma is the most spectacular and therefore the most travelled by visitors. But because the stark grandeur of the mountain chain and coast does not equate with physical comfort and hospitality, this part of Majorca is thinly populated, mainly by peasants who exist by the cultivation of olives, oranges, lemons and other fruit and engage in the traditional pattern of life which was evolved before mass markets were opened for their products. The gardens and orchards are usually terraced, while the entire length of coast facing Spain is broken in only a few places into accessible coves, inlets or harbours capable of catering for visitors, or even for the beach-lounger. Except in certain places below hillside villages where goat tracks or rudimentary roads zigzag their way to sea level, and at Puerto de Soller, where there is a sheltered harbour, and again at La Calobra where a 'torrent' disgorges into the sea, direct access is out of the question. The attraction lies in magnificent views from a well-engineered corniche which runs high above the cliffs for more than half the breadth of the island, from above the island of Dragonera in the south, before veering inland over the watershed and, still keeping to the heights, eventually ending at Cape Formentor in the extreme north.

While the sea along this coast is a compelling sight, with its deep blues streaked with the green of currents, and its lacy froth of waves fringing the rocks far below, the turns and twists of the coastal road bring equally impressive confrontations with the barren mountain peaks which on this exposed side of the island are particularly stark and forbidding. In fact they *are* some of them forbidden, because the highest of the range, Puig Mayor, has a radar station on its summit as part of the American Early Warning System. Though a road to the top has been created from what previously was a rough path, visitors are not allowed to use it except by special permit. This mountain, near the centre of the range which has eight others exceeding 1000 metres in height, rises to 1450 metres and stands less than 4 kilometres inland, a fact which proclaims its steepness. The public main road below it is in fact the continuation of the corniche which, coming in from the south, by-passes Soller before coiling around the side of the mountain to link with the route from Inca to La Colobra, and passes within a short distance of the famous Monastery of Lluch. This is one of the few routes through the mountains, though a circuitous one.

The easiest and most direct route to the coast from Palma is by the Soller road, which runs almost due north from the city. Other alternatives include an equally scenic drive by way of Valldemossa which reaches the coast south of Dejà, and another further south which crosses a broad pass near La Granja, to emerge not far from Bañalbufar. The self-driven visitor should beware of plotting journeys according to mileage, because the twists of these mountain and coastal roads add considerably to distances calculated in terms of a crow's flight, as well as imposing strain upon the driver. It is safer to plan practical round trips rather than to attempt to take in at one stretch the sights of a chain of mountains which, as the map shows, is little more that 100 kilometres in length and never more than 12 kilometres across, but which in fact occupies one-fifth of the island of Majorca. Failing a round tour, there is no monotony in driving to one place and back the same way, because the same spot seen from a different angle often offers views hidden the first time.

In any event, as the mountains are breached in only a few places, and hardly at all by secondary roads, alternatives are limited. One of the best round trips from Palma takes in the island's south-westerly corner, and after skirting Mount Galatzo on one of the most dramatic sections of the coast road, turns inland after Bañalbufar and climbs over one of the lower passes to descend to the plain through Esporlas. The distance by map reckoning is about 85 kilometres, but of course this does not take into account the possibility of being lured on one or other of the interesting detours which frequently occur before we strike the west coast, after which there are no alternatives except the possibility of driving on and making a wider sweep.

The populous part of the shores of the Bay of Palma are left behind after Palma Nova. Almost immediately there comes one of the decisions that have to be made on this part of the trip: whether to continue straight ahead, by-passing Magaluf and cutting across the neck of a small peninsula towards Santa Ponsa and Paguera, or to turn left and south on the secondary road leading to Cap de Cala Figuera and the attractive small seaside village of Portals Vells. If time is short and one continues westward, the road passes to the left of a shrine or *oratorio,* 16 kilometres from Palma, on a low pass known as La Coll de la Batalla, because it is here that it is believed the first mass was said to the troops of Jaime I, the Conquistador, after one of their first successful skirmishes following the historic landing. It incorporates a stone known as the Piedra Sagrada, which was used as a makeshift altar by the officiating bishop of Barcelona. A second reminder of this glorious series of events in the island's history comes at Santa Ponsa, or rather on its shoreline, which means taking a short detour to the left before reaching the town. Not only is the small promontory to the south one of the most successful areas of residential development, but it is here that Majorca's future king landed his invasion force, though he is believed to have previously set foot on Majorcan soil at the tiny island of Pantaleu, near San Telmo, only to decide that the rugged hinterland there would make a full-scale landing hazardous. The town of Santa Ponsa itself is sheltered, and was until fairly recently a place of old buildings and palm trees, but now it has been enlarged, mainly by blocks of flats. On the right above the town, where the road veers inland in order to cross the last open valley before the mountains and their ravines begin, one sees the great country house built by the Palmers who were among the four original families between whom the island was divided in the initial days of settlement.* Though in private hands now—actually under the ownership of the Credito Balearico Bank—it remains a landmark and a reminder of the method of land division formulated as a reward for loyalty in the provision of men and arms by noblemen without whom the landing could never have succeeded.

Paguera straggles a little, with hotels and distinct bathing beaches strung along the shore. Like many other resorts in this neighbourhood it is backed by dunes and pines, and seems to be a favourite with German and Scandinavian visitors. Small rocky islets within a short distance of the shore make for interesting swimming. One of the virtues of this place is that it, at last, appears to be self-sufficient and not dependent upon Palma for entertainment. In fact, most of the traffic is going the other way.

Excluding Camp de Mar, which has a tiny beach between two headlands and a small pier, the next place of importance is Andraitx, whose inland attractions happily do not greatly appeal to the sun and sea brigade. In fact it is one of the oldest settlements on the island, as is suggested by the Mallorquin 'x' in its name. The Romans called it Andrachium, and it became one of the classically fortified small towns or villages to be built some distance from the sea—in this case six kilometres from its natural port—as a defence against possible surprise attacks and ravages by Berber pirates. One of its old towers still exists. The town's atmosphere is particularly delightful. The streets are narrow and cobbled, overhung by tall thin houses, with doorways leading into cool patios. The predominant colour is a reddish brown, the local earth tint, with tiles to match, but many walls are colour-washed and sunburnt. The church is very old, dating in fact to the early thirteenth century, though a carving proclaims part of it as having been built in 1720.

Before exploring the nooks and crannies of Andraitx, there is hardly one of us who would not wish to linger in its charming little port. As it happens, a better idea than keeping to the inland road from Camp de Mar is to turn to the left there, where a signpost indicates Puerto d'Andraitx 4.4 kilometres. This side road leads over a pretty wooded hill, where villas have been introduced at different levels, and then descends rapidly to the quay. This really is a picture postcard place, and unspoilt since it is chiefly patronised by sailing folk, part-yachtsmen, part-native fishermen, making use of its jetties and excellent anchorage. Yachts of many nations tie up here, a good many flying the British ensign, and there are indications, such as pets aboard, to suggest that not all of these boats are used for sailing holidays, but double up as homes. There is ample space on the quays for sitting in the sun, watching the activity of others, while being served with food or drink from one of restaurants or bars across the road. Everything here is on a small scale, except the mountains dominated by Galatzo, immediately behind inland Andraitx. There is a second breakwater on the opposite side of the bay, offering other anchorages, and another lighthouse, as well as new houses fitted into the slopes in geometric patterns which do not detract from the prettiness of the scene. But as cliffs on both sides protect the entrance to the harbour, space for bathing is limited to one tiny beach near the port.

On the road back towards the town it may be noticed that this part of the island is truly rural in character. One sees waterwheels operated by mules, and communal open-air wash-houses where women gather. Before leaving the pleasant town of Andraitx it will be possible to take a second look at it, from its own level across the little valley. The main road seems to be heading straight for the mountains, but a way to the right

1 Inlet at Santa Ponsa, Majorca

2 Above. Bloodless bullfight, where young matadors are trained. Majorca

3 Top right. El Borne, Palma's main thoroughfare

4 Right. Folk Dancing at Selva, Majorca

9 Top left. Ferrerias, Minorca

10 Left. Harbour of the former capital Ciudadela, Minorca

11 The archway over Calle San Roque in the old part of Mahon, Minorca

12 Modern statue contrasting with the terrace houses in Mahon, Minorca

13 Above. Ibizan farmers' wives on their way to market

14 Above. An Ibizan shepherd woman

15 Right. Narrow white-washed streets in the old part of Ibiza town

16 Left. A typical windmill used to pump water from the deep wells, Ibiza

17 Above. Salt pans known as 'salinas' where salt is reclaimed from the sea by evaporation

18 Above. View. from La Mola lightouse on the eastern tip of Formentera

19 Top right. A San Fernando beach, Formentera

20 Right. The Romans named the island Formentera from their word for wheat, and wheat is still an important crop

21 Fishing and sailing in Formentera's one small harbour—La Sabina.
On the tree, fish drying in the sun

leads up after a few hundred yards to Son Mas, which is believed once to have been a Moorish castle. It would indeed have made an excellent defensive site, and its terrace has sturdy cannon to prove the point. From here there are fine views of sea one way and mountains the other, and of Andraitx and its church looking like a three-dimensional and neatly fitted together pile of children's bricks. Son Mas itself is the prototype of the grand Majorcan country home. It has an enormous courtyard equipped with a beautiful old wellhead, and stalls decorated with tiles and furnished with iron rings to which horses used to be tied. At the far end of the courtyard a well-proportioned staircase leads up to the *piano nobile,* which is bordered by arcades.

After descending again to the floor of the valley there is one more choice to be made. Almost thankfully, this is the last on offer before we launch ourselves inexorably upon a route which is neither straight nor narrow. This time the attraction is San Telmo, a small fishing village 7 kilometres to the west, and reached by driving first through citrus and olive groves shaded with the occasional carob tree, and then across the not very high Coll de S'Arraco. San Telmo has charm, and a sandy beach to match, as well as rocky coves to please the snorkeller. Though the village may be said to have come into existence only in the early nineteenth century, when the threat from Corsairs declined, its modern development began about 25 years ago. The saint after whom the place is named is that St Elmo who was martyred most unpleasantly—if martyrdom can ever be wholly pleasant—by having his intestines wound around a windlass. He is perhaps better known for St Elmo's fire, the corposant, or luminous ball of light which can accumulate on a ship's mast during an electric storm. In any event, the vicinity was historically remarkable for its part in the outer defence system of Andraitx, of which there remains a sixteenth century watchtower, and ruins of the original fort built in 1302 by Jaime II, and containing an oratory. Offshore, not more than 228 metres across a channel, we see the tiny island of Pantaleu, which was discarded by Jaime I as a landing place.

The much larger island of Dragonera is further away, across a channel which can seethe with turbulence, but otherwise is to be reached either by boat from Puerto d'Andraitx or San Telmo, or even by excursion trip from some of the resorts on Palma Bay. Its small harbour is on the landward side, and there is otherwise just a sprinkling of cottages and three lighthouses, the need for which becomes obvious should one be energetic enough to climb up 300 metres to the highest point of the island, which is in fact one chunk of limestone seven kilometres in length and, what is more critical, with 304 metres high cliffs dropping perpendicularly to seaward. To make the island even more of a hazard to mariners, this is the turning point in the approach to Palma. To sum up, Dragonera is for visitors endowed with time, energy and in picnicking mood. It is privately owned.

Meanwhile to return to the main route (if one has ever left it): the road was constructed early in the present century, and climbs steeply through pinewoods to reach an altitude of over 398 metres, a level which it maintains for some distance, with always glimpses of the sea far below on the left, and no prospect of driving down to it. It is understandable that there was no demand, earlier on, for a road from a scattered population which had little time for enjoyment of scenic grandeur. The mountains now press in so close that it is difficult for the motorist to see much except for their bare bones through which the road has been cut, and there is no village before Estèllenchs. However, here and there for the convenience of motorists, parking places have (literally) been engineered at points of the greatest magnificence, and some-times these are equipped with classic structures known by the beguiling name of *mirador*. The first of these, and one which complements one of the most spectacular views to be encoun-tered on this coast, is the Mirador de Ricardo Rocca, which justs out about 502 metres above a sheer drop to the sea, just before the road enters a short tunnel. There is also a good restaurant, set in a sort of eagle's eyrie to take advantage of the site, but the best views of all are obtained by going up the steps of the *mirador* itself, at the foot of which one may encounter women dressed in peasant costume, engaged in lace-making and selling this and other handicraft work particular to the region.

Not very long after passing through the tunnel, at another vantage point where there is a safe pull-in and a restaurant-cum-café at the Coll d'es Pi, the view includes the village of Estellènchs some distance below, and looking as though it has slid down the slopes of Mount Galatzo. This is a place of the senses; sights and the smell of warm pine needles, and particularly one may notice the sounds, coming through the clear mountain air, of people working in the terraces of olives and almond trees far below. From this height above the village it can be seen that the little beach belonging to it is some 152 metres below, and reached by a narrow road, little more than a crack in the cliff. It is a steep climb to undertake after a swim.

Estellènchs is dominated by its newly restored church with a square, flat-roofed belfry equipped with a charming sundial. But the greatest interest in these parts lies in the pockets of cultivation made possible by prodigious efforts on the part of man. The twin problems here were the conservation of soil and water. The earth could be contained within the massive walls of drystone terraces, built firmly according to the Roman technique, but the water had to be introduced. So channels were built to carry rainfall down the mountainside, for direct irrigation and for storage in cisterns. Some of these are covered as practised in the Moorish *vega* around Granada.

Not far beyond Estellènchs, when the road has swung back again to the top of the cliffs, there is a round watchtower overlooking the sea. The Atalaya de ses Animas, or the Tower of the Spirits, is representative of the chain of fifteenth and seventeenth century outposts built not so much for defence as part of an early warning system, by smoke and fire signals, which ringed the island so that the approach of an enemy could be circulated within a surprisingly short space of time. This particular one is the connecting link between Dragonera and the entrance to Soller harbour.

If ever a series of views can truthfully be said to beggar description, those of this Majorcan coast do just that, with the combination of bare mountain, sheer cliffs, grotesque rock shapes and areas of cultivation graced by old country houses, more mansions than farmhouses, fit for the accommodation of the wealthy. Where the frame of the mountain has been sheered away to make passage for our road, the rockface is often decorated with long, dripping stalactites, with brilliant ferns in every crevice.

The next village, Bañalbufar, provides a contrast to Estellènchs. For one thing, it is more open to the sea, and built in tiers to correspond with the terraced land around it. For another, it is almost completely treeless. But it is a place of great beauty, surrounded by terraces of such height and width as are seldom seen elsewhere, their crops an emerald green, thanks again to the expert provision of a water supply. The method here depends upon large cisterns, open to the sky, attached to almost every house, even in the village itself. Tomatoes are one of the main crops of the district, though once upon a time its vineyards were celebrated for sweet wine made from Malvasia grapes, similar to the Malmsey of the Canaries and Madeira. But the estate from which it came is now a hotel. Ways down to the sea from Bañalbufar do exist, but they are as steep as that from Estellènchs. There are hotels, and the place is a favourite with walkers, who however, have not much level ground at their disposal, and must therefore be prepared to take to the mountain paths.

Bañalbufar is near a turning point. Our road twists inland and upward, out of sight of the sea, and after nine kilometres, at a fork marked L for Valldemossa, the right fork is the one to take for a return towards Palma. This leads past the great estate of La Granja, the 'grange', once owned by the Cistercian fraternity in Palma. Subsequently what had been their sheep farm was acquired by the noble Fortuny family, who built a fine seventeenth century residence set among gardens equipped with the luxury of running water and connecting ponds—all in a superb style of landscaping. The place is now open to the public, and is well worth visiting, not only for its garden, pergolas and walks, but also for the house itself, which is approached through a courtyard with a fountain, and which has a balustraded front, the roof being supported by arches on slender pillars to reproduce a distinctly Moorish flavour. As the house looks out over a steep slope, its back is of one storey only. This place is a tourist attraction, not only for the beauty of its setting, but because it has been turned into a centre for traditional arts and handicrafts, where regular folk-dancing performances are staged.

After passing La Granja we have crossed the watershed, and the view of the Bay of Palma and the plain behind the city come into sight. The descent is made by easy gradients, passing through Esporlas and its orange groves, then Establiments, before reaching the suburbs which inevitable accompany a city. On the way one glimpses numerous fine country houses attached to estates which are still in the ownership of many of Majorca's aristocracy and descendants of her merchant princes.

A second drive through the mountains touches coastal scenery which is scarcely less magnificent. In this instance there is a certain amount of more recent history, clinging particularly to the memory two men and one woman—foreigners all—who left their mark upon this part of the island. The story of the three months' stay of George Sand, the French novelist, and Frederic Chopin at Valldemossa has overlaid that spot with an extra veneer of mystique, as though the old monastery built on the site of an ancient palace were not romantic enough in its own right to attract coachloads of visitors. On the other hand, the achievements of the Archduke Luis Salvador of Austria, are less well-known. He bought land and formed great estates all around the cliffbound coast, setting palatial houses in lands made fertile. His preoccupation with all things Majorcan deserves attention in another chapter, together with the stories of some of the greatest Majorcans who in days gone by made an important contribution to the world at large.

If travelling clockwise, one leaves Palma by the Soller road, taking almost immediately a left fork for Valldemossa. At first the land is level, and devoted primarily to the cultivation of almonds, but as soon as it begins to rise these trees are superseded by citrus, and then by olives. These lovely, romantic trees are an important part of the landscape, as well as having been the main livelihood of the local people in the days before tourism drew a drift of wage-earners away from the soil. Some of these trees, with their contorted branches and hollow trunks reminiscent of Arthur Rackham's illustrations for Grimms' Fairytales are believed to be nearly 1000 years old. Two places to look out for the best specimens are above Esglaietas on this road, and then again overlooking the coast. Esglaietas has a glass factory at which visitors are welcome to watch the blowers at work.

After the village, about 12 kilometres from Palma, the road begins to climb and soon the foothills yield to high mountains which have a kind of tidemark at an altitude where pines and bare rock take over from the olives. The road squeezes between cliffs, then continues its way above a fertile valley, to where, 17 kilometres from Palma, and 400 metres above sea level, the village of Valldemossa enjoys a temperate climate. It is this freshness in the air which first attracted King Sancho to the place in 1311, at a time when the accommodation for royalty was little more than a hunting lodge. But he found relief here from the asthma which afflicted him in his palace of the Almudaina.

In 1339 Sancho's successor, Martin of Aragon, gave the palace to Carthusian monks from Tarragona in Catalonia. Their new foundation came to be known as La Real Cartuja, or the Royal Charterhouse. Though little remains from those early days, the monastic buildings form a tranquil group set amongst trees—palms and cypresses—but overlooked at some distance by barren conical hills which themselves are over-shadowed by mountains. The views, far and near, are superb. A supply of undergound water which collects in cavities below porous rock are the key to the luxuriance of the terraced gardens.

The Carthusian monks were expelled from Majorca in 1835, and though members of the fraternity who had fled from

Spain at the same time were able eventually to return to the mother house on the mainland, Valldemossa was never re-occupied as a living community. However, some venerable monks had contrived to linger on unobtrusively, one of them serving the village and neighbourhood as a pharmacist. The oldest surviving parts of the monastery, notably the cloister dedicated to St Mary the Virgin, date from the seventeenth century, but the church and the convent cloister were built some hundred years later. The monks lived in small cells, but larger rooms en suite, were apportioned to the Prior and other important clerics. These particular cells, which range along one side of the cloisters in sets of three rooms apiece, are spacious and possess small individual gardens, complete with topiary work and running water. It was here that in the winter of 1838–9 Chopin, George Sand and her two children came to live, in what proved to be a stormy and ill-conceived interlude in their love affair. Similarly, but surely more appropriately, sets of rooms are nowadays leased to private individuals. The full story of what turned out to be a series of contretemps is told amusingly by Robert Graves, whose house is not far from here, and rather more one-sidedly by the authoress herself in her *Winter in Majorca*. It has been translated into many other languages besides the French in which it was written.

Though not of great antiquity, the neo-classical church possesses interesting details, including lovely floor tiles and frescoes in the vaulted ceiling which were painted by a Carthusian monk who happened to be the brother-in-law of the painter Goya. Other interesting things to look for include the choir stalls, and the Pieta of the High Altar. The sacristy contains reliquaries, embroidered vestments and an interesting plaster altar screen.

Though it is only an adjunct, many people will find the pharmacy of the monastery the most memorable feature. This was equipped in 1723, and remains unchanged as a mini-museum displaying, as though in current use, many of the old medicaments in containers of Majorcan glass and ceramic jars from Barcelona—most of which were actually being used until the last survivor of the monastic druggists died in 1853. After that date the village pharmacist, a layman, continued to occupy the premises, and worked behind these same counters using the old tools of his trade. The little shop operated until 1912.

The prior's quarters, which include a private chapel and a library, are shown to the public. Unfortunately, however, when they fled from Valldemossa the monks took most of their possessions away with them, so that the furniture on display, though of the correct period, is not the original, though the books and manuscripts in the library are.

When we come to the rooms occupied by George Sand, her lover and their small entourage, the same applies. The furniture, though right, is not actually what was used by the famous couple, the exception being Chopin's piano, which had created so much disturbance in the attempt to get it up the mountain that it had to be abandoned. A fresh rose is placed on its keyboard every day. But though the furniture was not theirs, manuscripts belonging to both, portraits and some of Chopin's personal possessions brought from Poland fill rooms which are slightly claustrophobic, so that it is a relief to step outside into the formal little gardens, one to each room, to lean over the balustrade to enjoy the view, to smell the flowers, and to listen to the tinkle of running water.

Unfortunately the legend which has fastened upon this place attracts visitors in such numbers that they have to be passed in multi-lingual batches through those parts of the monastery which are open to the public. As a 'finale', exhibitions of folk-dancing are given for the visitors in an adjacent building known as King Sancho's Palace. The local peasant costume, which includes a coif of Majorcan lace framing their faces in an oval, is particularly becoming to the women, as are the baggy trousers and cummerbunds of the men. The dances often have a vocal accompaniment. Local handicrafts, including the traditional lace, are on sale outside.

The village of Valldemossa is usually less crowded than the monastery. Its streets are narrow and winding and full of flowers—thanks again to a plentiful supply of water. This is the birthplace of Majorca's own saint, Catalina Tomàs, whose house is open to visitors.

Hardy walkers, who need not actually be climbers, can make an expedition from here to the summit of Teix (1064 metres). A well-marked route passes Son Gual and Sa Comar, two minor properties once owned by the Archduke Luis Salvador. Close to the summit the ridge flattens out for a stretch of about one kilometre. The last 200 metres is trackless, because the path below it now begins to swing down the Soller side of the mountain. This means that one has to clamber over rough ground to reach the so-called King Jaime's Chair of stone, from which almost the entire island may be surveyed. It is said that the suffering King Sancho habitually had himself carried to this high throne, as here if anywhere the thin mountain air would relieve his breathing.

By road, the watershed is crossed a short distance above Valldemossa, where the gap between mountains is wider than at comparable passes north or south. The sea soon comes into view. After descending to the level of what is almost a plateau running in a strip above the cliffs, we take a fork to the right for Dejà, instead of turning south in the direction of Bañalbufar. This can be claimed to be the Archduke's territory. Not only did he conceive stately houses and cultivate his lands, but he also adorned salient points along the coast with classical *miradors*. One of these, the Ses Pites, at the 21st kilometre mark from Palma, is typical. All are worth stopping for. At this point too there is a road up to the right leading to La Ermita (the hermitage), a religious outpost, on one of the few permissible turnings off the coast road. Travellers are welcome, even if they have only come to picnic in the shade of the trees.

Miramar is the first of the Archduke's more important houses to be reached. He built it on the site of what had been Ramon Llull's school of Arabic studies, and in the grounds there is a cave which that medieval scholar and traveller is presumed to have used when at work or in meditation. The small commemorative chapel nearby dates from 1876, and the archway in the garden comes from the Convent of Santa Magdalena in Palma. Miramar, which one hesitates to translate as 'Seaview', also has its *mirador,* close to a seventeenth century watchtower about 500 metres further along the road.

Then, only about 2 kilometres further on, we come to Son Marriog, the second of the great properties owned by the Archduke. This one is open to the public, and contains paintings, furniture and collections reflecting and owner's catholic tastes: archaeology, geology, natural history and almost all natural sciences are represented, and do something to explain why this foreign nobleman elected to spend some 50 years of his life on the island. The *mirador* here takes the form of a charming belvedere in white Carrara marble. It perches above a steep precipice overhanging the small promontory of Na Forradada far below, which is pierced by a natural tunnel 110 ft in width in which the Archduke habitually moored his yacht.

Dejà is the next village. As with the others, it is sited halfway down the mountain slope. The road descends to its level through terraces of particularly old and gnarled olives. So steep is the hill on which Dejà is built that its houses have to derive their support from arches which span the village streets. This is perhaps the most widely renowned of the coastal villages, at least to foreigners, who have acquired a great many houses here. It has in fact become something of an artists' and writers' colony, amongst whom Robert Graves has contributed much to its repute. The peak of Teix looms behind, and there is a steep track leading to the sea. The smaller hamlet of Lluch Alcari, a short distance to the north, rivals Dejà in picturesqueness.

Our road continues to twist and turn even after it has veered inland to join the direct route from Palma to Soller, and while it descends we get an excellent view of Soller's intensively cultivated valley, an amphitheatre flanked by mountains, including Puig Mayor, the highest of them all. The name of the town derives from the Arabic *sulliar,* meaning golden. There are tiny villages to be identified, and perhaps visited later, and it will be seen that the slopes are speckled with small houses in evergreen plantations of oranges.

As usual in these parts, the town's port is some distance away from the prosperous town. But what is not usual is that the two are connected by a most intriguing tramway, which runs from Soller's railway station to the quays.

Puerto de Soller, guarded by twin lighthouses, is almost landlocked, but remains true to its name, as may be seen by the number of fishing-boats in the harbour, and the nets spread out to dry on the seaward side of its one street. In fact this was already a village in 1231 at the time of the second landing by Jaime II. It is a most happy place to linger, and there are any amount of shops selling lace, olive-wood carvings, clothing made of the hide of kids, and the local Majorcan lace, as well as, of course, a choice of eating places on the waterfront.

The town of Soller itself looks inward towards the mountains, and has no view of the sea, a sign that it relied upon its outpost to warn of danger from pirates. As it happens, invading Turks did get through in 1561, but were defeated, though unfortunately only after they had pillaged the town. This event is celebrated by a Victory Feast early in May, and the enactment of a spirited battle between Turks and Christians. As Majorcan towns go, Soller is quite large, and once was exceedingly prosperous as the centre of a flourishing export business which was already famous in the sixteenth century. Wealth gained from the citrus trade and other forms of horticulture made it possible for the citizens to finance the narrow gauge railway between their town and Palma. This cuts through the solid rock of the mountain at a high level in a series of tunnels and it is an ideal way to travel. The first-class 'parlour cars' can take one, not only through glorious scenery, but into another world, which is still not too near modernity by the time one emerges at the town's old-fashioned station. The tram terminus, the neo-Gothic church of San Bartolomé—which

houses a beautiful fourteenth-century Madonna and a statue of
the patron saint in black marble—and a pleasant town square
with fountain and restaurants, are only a few steps downhill.

The atmosphere of the town is vaguely French, due perhaps
to the traditional commercial traffic between here and Marseilles, which encouraged Soller's emigrants to set up as merchants
in the more prosperous Midi of France, before returning home
a good deal wealthier than when they left. This is a pleasant
place to stay for people who are not completely sold upon
being able to step straight from their hotel into the sea. It can
be particularly recommended to walkers, even to those unwil-
ling or unable to scale heights. A few villages, all of them
enchanting, are within easy reach on foot or by horse-drawn
carriage. Fornalutx is the easiest to get to, by a road that
follows the bed of a river. Its streets become flights of irregular
steps, flowers spill over the patios and are ranged outside the
grilles of windows, and it has a nice plain church which stands
at the head of more steps. Biniaraitx and Binibassi are two
smaller hamlets typical of hillside communities which have
been blessed with water, soil, shelter and natures industrious
enough to ensure a decent livelihood. Then there are more
strenuous excursions which may be taken to a canyon or two,
and towards the sea. Failing that, there is always the tram, or
some intermediate journey on the train.

The return journey to Palma by road leads over the Soller
Pass, at an altitude of nearly 914 metres, after which the
descent is fairly gradual, and made in a series of giant curves
rather than hairpin bends, so that there are opportunities for
admiring the inland views and the bay beyond the city.

There are two more possible places to visit as part of the
descent to the level of the plain and what may be called the
almond-growing level. First, on the left of the road and marked
by a splendid avenue of plane trees, we come to the Alfabia
estate. This property was originally owned by a rich Moor who
collaborated with Jaime I, and it was subsequently acquired by
a noble Majorcan family. One of the secrets of the beauty of
the gardens is the plentiful supply of water, used both for the
irrigation of the gardens and their embellishment by fountains
and channels running from one level to another. Even so, the
Arabian Nights' atmosphere depends as much upon the shade
thrown by tall trees as upon the roses and jasmine that scent
the air. Fresh orange and lemon juice is sold in a pavilion near
the bottom of the gardens. The house is arranged as a
museum, and it contains typically Majorcan furniture and
ceramics, and houses a library. The few Moorish remains to be

seen are the coffered ceiling of the gatehouse, inlaid with rare woods, and an inscription in Arabic over the entrance. But perhaps the most evocative reminder of its origins is the enormous courtyard with its central tree and geometrical patterns in cobblestones.

There is another fine house, 12 kilometres from Palma, after Buñola. This is indeed as much a castle as a house, complete with landscaped gardens which are worth visiting now or on a separate trip from Palma. Raixa came into the possession of the aristocratic Despuig family in 1620, but the present house was built by the most notable member of that family, Cardinal Despuig, at the end of the eighteenth century. Again there is a well-shaded courtyard as the approach to the great yellow stone house. But the main feature of the estate is undoubtedly the great Italianate flight of steps modelled on those of the Villa d'Este near Florence, and which has statuary and fountains to either side, with cypresses also standing sentinel. At the top there is a statue brought from Rome, one of the collection made by the Cardinal. Others have since been removed to museums. The climb is worthwhile—though many, the steps are shallow—because it leads in the direction of a lovely man-made lake which provides water which courses down innumerable irrigation channels.

The remainder of the route passes through orchards, and runs parallel to the Soller-Palma railway. The city is entered through the Avenida de Soller.

The third way through the mountains is by its highest pass, which involves if not difficult at least tiring driving, so that it might be a good plan to consider either being chauffeur-driven or else joining an organized party. Picture postcards of the road to La Calobra and the Torrente de Pareis confirm this, since they show the road winding so tortuously that in one place it coils round under itself like a boa constrictor. On the other hand, in favourable weather, which means a calm sea, it is possible to hire a boat in Puerto de Soller, so as to disembark far up the calanque at the mouth of the spectacular *torrente*. Or a similar boat trip may be taken from Cala de San Vicente, an attractive resort off the road north of Pollensa. However this would mean missing the experience of cutting through rock and mountain, as well as a visit to the Monastery of Lluch, high in the mountains. This establishment differs considerably from Valldemossa, being not so much a showplace as a working religious house, with a long history as a place of pilgrimage.

Approaching from the direction of Palma, we take the

Pollensa road, the straightness of which, below the mountain range, suggests a Roman origin, as a link between their two settlements. Just over halfway, we turn left at Inca, heading into a wall of mountains, and towards the intriguing silhouette of Selva, a small town on a low ridge. In the manner of similar country churches, the Iglesia San Lorenzo is arcaded at a level above the falling ground, and looks as though it has been pinned into place by its square tower. Though built in the thirteenth century, it was restored in 1855 after having been damaged by fire. Forty-two steps lead up to its west front, with companion cypresses, opposite the *plaza* dedicated to General Primo de Rivera. Open-air folk dancing displays are held in the square during the season, usually on Tuesday and Friday afternoons.

The next village to be reached is on the left of the road. Caimari is reputed to produce the finest quality olive oil in the island. After leaving it on the left the mountains begin in earnest, and soon the road has ascended from near sea level to the 379 metres Colle de Guz by what have been counted as 150 serpentine twists. This is a land of irregular terraces with olives clinging tenaciously to stony soil. When terracing peters out there are evergreen oaks, then scrubby pines and, eventually naked rock. It hardly needs emphasizing that there are splendid views on all sides—a further indication that the responsible chauffeur does not have an enviable role.

After a rock cutting, with scree and shale on either side to follow, another mountain road turns off for Pollensa and, almost immediately for a side turning to the monastery. However, should one continue towards La Calobra, intending perhaps to visit the monastery on the return journey, there is a safe pull-in near a stone cross, from which one has an almost aerial view of the entire group of monastic buildings, looking from this height like a Leggo construction. The whole of this district was granted to the Knights Templar in acknowledgement of their part in the Reconquest. Initially the Christian community was served by the chapel of San Pedro at Escorca, nearer the coast. This is believed to be the first church to have been built after the settlement, but this use of the little church declined with the growth of the monastery, which was founded in the fourteenth century. The story goes that a peasant boy happened by accident upon the carved image of a beautiful woman. When this discovery was investigated by one of the Escorca monks, he had a vision of a phantom crown suspended in the heavens, and heard sweet music. The image was identified as that of the Blessed Virgin Mary, and a shrine was

built. By 1430 an Augustinian monastery had been established
in the sacred place, with a seminary for boys attached. Vocal
and instrumental music, theology, Castilian and Latin were the
principal studies. Nowadays the school is run by the Order of
the Sacred Heart, and the buildings, which have been vastly
expanded and restored, almost beyond recognition, include a
guesthouse for parents and others wishing to stay, some
self-contained apartments let by the week, and a refectory for
casual visitors. It is a pleasant place, with out-buildings giving
the impression of a well-run farm, and all set in a serene
environment.

The seventeenth-century church makes good use of red
marble, and is decorated throughout, making it rather oppres-
sive, but its side chapel, though modern, is of greater
importance for the reason that it contains the small statue of
Nuestra Señora de Lluch or, as she is more familiarly known,
La Morenata, meaning the Little Brown One. The image
stands behind the altar, though it is carried through to the
church on special occasions. There are steps leading up which
allow a more detailed inspection of the medieval representation
of Mother and Christ Child, whose heads are framed by
intricate golden haloes. It does not detract from the beauty of
this statue, and perhaps lends a further element of myserty to
it, that though the antiquity of the little Virgin is never in
doubt, she has a rival. An alabaster figure which came into the
hands of a Majorcan merchant in 1518 is counter-claimed to be
the true one originally discovered by the Arab shepherd
somewhere in the vicinity of the present avenue of plane trees.

The monastery's museum contains a wide variety of exhibits,
many of which have been tendered as gifts, explaining the
random nature of the collections. There are coins, flints, fans,
musical instruments, pottery, vestments, jewellery and various
primitive tableaux, as far as possible arranged according to
kind and chronology.

Returning to the commemorative cross on the main road, we
begin to climb again through wooden country. Nowadays the
village of Escorca contains little more than a cluster of houses,
but is remarkable not only for its chapel, but as a preliminary
viewpoint of the extraordinary scenery which has brought us
here. For the first time it is possible to look down into the
fearsome miniature Grand Canyon formed in early ages by
melted snow rushing down from Puig Mayor and its sister
mountains. A good head for heights is needed here and at a
belvedere further along the road, where one leans out over
jagged, hostile rocks. There are two more passes to be

negotiated, one of them reaching an altitude of 719 metres until, after passing a roadside bar and an aqueduct carrying spring water, followed by a tunnel cut into pinnacled rocks, we meet the road from Soller. This has followed the course of rivers rising on the great mountain's eastern slope. Incidentally it is from this route that the road leads to the summit of Puig Mayor and the white domes of the tracking station that sit on it.

From the junction of the two roads onwards the descent to the coast becomes very steep indeed, involving a series of convolutions through jagged rocks which are devoid even of the great clumps of Mediterranean heath, bracken, bright lichens and other growth which have coloured the roadside clefts at the higher altitude. Then suddenly the occasional homely farm is seen from above, with the dark green of its citrus foliage contrasting with the lunar landscape enclosing it. At last, after passing a rock pinnacle known as Cavali Bernat and a side turning to Tuent, a new development area, sea level is reached.

La Calobra is a tiny place, with minimal hotel accommodation though a handful of café-bars and souvenir shops. The many visitors who by one method or another have managed to get here can walk without difficulty along the edge of the Torrente de Pareis on a path tunnelled through the cliff in 1950. This exploration-made-easy takes about 20 minutes, but when the path comes to an end, things become more difficult. It is a matter of negotiating a way over banks of shingle, with some paddling or even swimming thrown in, or by traversing the rocks. There are always pools, even when the flow of the river has ceased in summer, except during times of occasional thunderstorm and spate. Hardier people still, if they have about six hours at their disposal, may attempt the exacting expedition right up the crack of the canyon, where cliffs rise sheer to a height of 309 metres. This would bring them (with a guide) to below Escorca, where at last it is possible to climb out of the abyss. But this exercise needs stamina, the sure feet of a mountain goat, and readiness to take to the water. However, let it be said that it is unnecessary to feel forced to negotiate the course of the *torrente* 'just because it is there', since the mixture of cliffs, blue sea and greenish fresh water is at its prettiest, if not its most dramatic in its lower reaches. Without doubt this is an idyllic place.

5 Inside Majorca

Certainly the market towns of the plain have little in common with Sodom and Gomorrah. But that is how I think of Majorca's inland places, perhaps because there is something biblical about them. Their principal feature is almost invariably a church, the fruits of the earth are on sale in their markets, and in the simple, rolling countryside surrounding them one occasionally glimpses a working camel amongst the wells and windmills, and frequent processions of field workers commuting on foot or donkey-back between the fields and the traditional security of tightly circumscribed communities.

No part of an island as small as Majorca can expect to remain unvisited and inviolate. Yet, thankfully, there are always for one reason or another features which pass or are passed unnoticed. And this is particularly true of the inland districts, through which traffic hurtles at speed from coast to coast, and where the pre-ordained halts are factories-cum-souvenir-shops—a schedule which allows very little time for individual exploration. Whether it be north, south, east or west the sea draws visitors like a magnet along no more than three highways: between Palma and Pollensa/Alcudia in the north, the opposite tip of the island where the secondary range of mountains ends in steep precipices near Artà, and another less travelled road leading to the more southerly *calas* of the east coast. But along these three routes respectively, we pass through Santa Maria, Binissalem and Inca; Algaida, Montuiri, Villafranca and Manacor; Lluchmayor and Campos—while between the last two, and not to be disregarded, is Felanitx. Each of these towns has close ties with villages which may be off the tourist map but which are pleasant to visit, as typical of an older Majorca.

Manacor is Majorca's second largest and most important town, as well as being the most industrial, though its factories rely a great deal upon craftsmanship as opposed to mechanical processes, in providing for 28,000 or more inhabitants. It also has an older tradition as a market centre catering for the country districts of the south-east, hints of which are revealed on the latter half of the 48 kilometre route from Palma, which passes through a procession of almond orchards, fig plantations, vineyards, vegetable plots and cereal-growing land. As a historic town founded by Jaime II on the site of a Moorish settlement, and not far from the Roman Cunium, Manacor has just a few ancient buildings remaining. These include the Torre de Palau, part of a royal palace which was in fact little more than a fortified town house. A corresponding survivor of the town's defensive system is the fifteenth-century Torre de Ses Puntas, which incorporates an example of the typical Gothic window known as a *finestra coronelle,* and more importantly, houses an interesting archaeological museum, which contains among other things a collection of ancient coins found in the neighbourhood.

The church's tall bell tower, looking deceptively like a minaret, can be seen for miles ahead when approaching from the west. But the seventeenth–eighteenth-century cloister should be sought out. Then, much older still, and a few miles out of town at Son Pereto there are the remains of a Roman civic building which was converted into later use as a Christian basilica, the mosaics of which have been removed for safe keeping to the museum. These things are played down by the local people, and by the tourist authorities, so that the coaches which stop for an hour or so rather arbitrarily channel their customers into one or other of Manacor's well-publicised artificial pearl factories. These visits are interesting and well organized, so that by walking along the production line through a series of corridors it is possible to witness the birth of pearls which have became known in world markets, but which have not arisen, like Aphrodite from the sea. The details of the process—or rather the materials of which they are made—are a jealously guarded trade secret, though it is hinted that pulverised fish scales are one of the basic ingredients. What one sees is the series of firing and polishing and grading processes, done by girls on the other side of glass screens, showing what look like sticks of opaque sealing wax being melted to take the shape of a globule transfixed on the end of a steel wire, held by hand and twiddled dexterously near a flame to reach the required perfection of form. The pearls themselves and jewellery made from them, may be bought in adjacent showrooms and also in Palma and elsewhere. The other products manufactured in this town and its neighbourhood are less easy to carry home: furniture, pots and roof tiles, all of excellent workmanship and owing a great deal to traditional methods.

Inca, 20 kilometres along the road from Palma to Pollensa and Alcudia, is the other important industrial town. It specialises in leatherwork, shoemaking and textiles, but though growing in size to rival Manacor it is also a busy agricultural centre. The traffic is two-way, because lorry-loads of workers commute there every day. Its Thursday market is famous, and features on most tourist programmes, while the November agricultural fair attracts a great deal of general interest, even though increasingly the accent is upon farm machinery. A sign of the times is that many town houses have been demolished and replaced by commercial buildings. Like many another, the church of Santa Maria la Mayor was built in the eighteenth century and has a neo-Gothic bell tower, with the traditional cloisters attached. It does not occupy the site of the original church, which grew out of a mosque adapted for Christian usage, and which was later to become the convent of San Bartolomé, but the main feature to look for is its Renaissance altar backed by a Madonna portrayed against a gold background. Another easily identifiable building is the convent of San Jeronimo, where the sisters make a very special Majorcan cake known as *concos d'Inca*. Incidentally, this is something of a gourmet's town, because not only are the wine districts close at hand, but the skills of local cookery or *cocina tipica* are exercised in converted wine vaults, such as in the ancient Son Fuster Inn, where such delicacies as roast suckling pig and baby lamb delicately flavoured with mountain herbs may be ordered and enjoyed.

Most of the smaller towns on cross-country routes have some individual interest, and warrant at least a casual halt. Since they are few enough, no difficult decisions are involved. For instance, the road running north-east from Palma through Inca first passes Santa Maria, then Consell, where the making of *alpargetas* or esparto grass sandals is a cottage industry, then Binissalem, which makes red wine judged to be the best in the country. The best for easy sightseeing, unless buying or imbibing specifically, must be Santa Maria, only 15 kilometres from Palma, and linked by a frequent bus service. Wines may also be sampled at a bodega settled deep into the arcades of the former convent of Minimos. Another sixteenth-century convent, dedicated to Santa Maria de la Real, is next to the local museum, which specialises in natural history. Then the parish church, in a side street has doors in the baroque style which is repeated by the Town Hall. However, to my mind the most beautiful thing in this old town—which rather suffers from being on a busy road—is a fifteenth-century painting in the church, depicting the Madonna and the boy Jesus, who holds a goldfinch lightly by a thread. It is pleasant to see such things in their rightful place, instead of removed to a museum or art gallery, where their significance may be somewhat diminished.

The name of Binissalem with its Moorish connotations is as attractive as its wine, which is on tap for all comers. This is one of the market towns which were founded by Jaime II in 1300 to become an agricultural centre for the neighbouring estates which had been handed over to seigneurial families. Many fine houses off the main street reflect that tradition, though none survive from the original period. But the church was founded in 1364, when it was built in the prevalent Catalan-Gothic style, only to be largely rebuilt in the eighteenth century, and added to later. The dome is octagonal and has a central lantern tower at its east end, while the interior has lavish marble decoration.

The much travelled road between Palma and Manacor which leads to the east coast, bypasses intervening towns, eventually to reach Artà. Short detours from it will reveal Alguida as a quaint little old-fashioned town, with narrow streets and shuttered houses which seem to argue that the population is mysteriously indoors, whereas in reality nearly everyone is out working in the fields. Then there is Montuiri, on a ridge to the left of the road. It has special fascination because the rising ground where it stands is studded with largely disused windmills which since their sails and caps have crumbled take on the appearance of a series of watchtowers. There are also the ruins of a medieval convent. Villafranca, nearer Manacor, is dominated by the dome of its church, surmounted by a gigantic statue of the Christ.

Artá, in the east, is a small town of distinct personality, and the feeling is that it is fortunate in not attracting too much attention from visitors hell-bent on getting to the sea or the caves which burrow deep into the headlands. In fact the town is sufficiently off the main road to give it a measure of immunity, even though, being on a hill, it is clearly visible. This part of the country was settled very early in the island's history. Evidence of this exists in the form of numerous *talayots* or miniature Stonehenges, such as Ses Paisses south of the town, and Sa Canova on the road to Alcudia. The town of Artá later became a Phoenician trading post, after which, when occupied by the Moors it was known as Jartan. It still has the appearance of a typical medieval hill town, with a dominant position on rising ground which eventually becomes the rocky, almost trackless north-east corner of the island. The castle and immense church

of Puig de San Salvador dominate the town, and an outline of
its walls can still be traced. But amongst the chief fascinations,
to my mind, are the old, solid houses lining its winding paved
streets. Some have the coats of arms of the nobility on their
façades, and others lintels and doorposts of black marble. The
castle makes a good grandstand from which to overlook the
district, and there is an archaeological museum containing
finds from local excavations, including some Punic or Carthaginian artefacts, which are scarcer on this island than in Ibiza.

There are alternative routes from Palma to the *calas* of the
south-east coast. One passes the airport, and leads directly to
Lluchmayor, a town which serves a countryside known to have
been settled many years before the advent of the Romans. The
other at first skirts the Bay of Palma to seaward of the narrow
strip of high-rise development which culminates in Arenal, after
which the coast becomes rocky, and sheers off to the south.
Though the most logical route is to turn inland here for
Lluchmayor, the alternative is to follow the coast along the cliffs
which though not nearly as high as those of the west, are only
breached in a few places. This is a direction to take if one wishes to
wander, rather than to embark upon planned sightseeing,
though there is one exception in the prehistoric remains of
Capicorp Vey, which is just off a secondary road between Cabo
Blanco and Lluchmayor. These megalithic monuments are
complete enough to be impressive, as well as unique as far as this
island is concerned. The key to the village, or fortress—it is not
known for sure which it was—is to be found at a farmhouse just
across the road from the entrance, and a booklet attempts to
explain the mysteries which are still in dispute among
archaeologists.

Lluchmayor is a lively inland town, where shoemaking was once
an important means of livelihood, but where the making of jams
and other preserves has now taken over. The fruit-growing
neighbourhood depends upon irrigation. Midway between
Lluchmayor and Villafranca a secondary road leads through
wheat-growing country where once there used to be armies of
working windmills, to Porreras which has a church famous for its
art treasures, amongst which is a processional cross originally the
property of the Knights Templar.

Felanitx has a reputation for its good white wine. It also has a
large church, built in the twelfth century, but restored in the
seventeenth. As this is a hill district, water is more plentiful, and
the town can afford a handsome fountain in its central *plaza*.

All these towns are on the way somewhere, in fact to resorts where there are restaurants and hotels and shops, but some inland villages, especially those to the north of centre, really manage to lie off the tourist map. They belong completely to the countryside, and it to them, and it is advisable to seek them out on some aimless, meandering tour, rather than in the helter-skelter of a point-to-point. Some of the most interesting are in the triangle made by the Bay of Alcudia and the main roads from Palma to Alcudia and Manacor. Often their differences are explained by history and the type of agricultural land upon which they depend.

Sineu, originally the Moorish town of Sixneu, has a church which was built from a converted mosque, a fact not unusual in the early days of the Reconquest. And indeed the balcony around the pyramidical belfry does vaguely suggest a minaret. The convent of the Immaculada grew out of the royal residence or Alcazar—hence the designation of what is now a secondary road to Palma as 'royal'. This market town is also responsible for the manufacture of a fiery spirit, *aguardiente,* so be warned.

Muro has an interesting ethnological museum, with a specialised collection of agricultural implements which it is interesting to compare and contrast with those now employed in a intensively horticultural district.

La Puebla is of special interest because of its foundation as a peasant community by Jaime I, for the benefit of those Catalan supporters who were prepared to settle on the land. The church is tall, the buildings and streets are laid out, rather unusually, in a grid, and windmills abound as part of the drainage system necessary for the marshy ground on which it lies, some of which is still cropped by hemp for use in the weaving of baskets, hats and matting. The village comes to life, or returns to olden days, on St James's Day, 25 June, when there is cavorting by masked 'giants' around bonfires.

Then, on the northern side of the Palma-Alcudia road, and owing greater allegiance to the mountains than the lower pastoral land, we find Lloseta, not far from Inca, where there is a splendid palace, now restored, in the present ownership of the March family. Campanet is not far away, and has not only a complex of caves but a typical medieval church which has suffered less than most from restoration. Indeed, most of the countryside in these parts is beautiful, unspoilt and productive.

6 Celebrities, Castles and Calvaries

It often happens that a little knowledge of eminent men gives one some insight into the character of the country from which, or to which, they came. Looking back into the history of Majorca one sees the conquistadores who built castles and formed great estates, scholars and cartographers who travelled the world and often came home to rest, and monks and missionaries who continue to inspire deep religious feeling.

The warriors, of course, came first, and built not only the Castle of Bellver but strongholds guarding all the coasts and mountain passes. Apart from the purely functional watchtowers, many of the castles doubled up as country residences for the kings of Majorca. All are now in disrepair, but because of their dominant situation there is sure to be an excellent view, and they make good places for picnics. Another thing is that because of the time involved in climbing to them by tracks which can be rough, they tend to be visited only by independent sightseers. Most of the sites had been occupied by the Moors before the island was wrested from their hands.

Alaro Castle is two-three kilometres from the village of that name, to the left of the road leading north and then east to the village of Orient. When first seen, its masonry, of local stone blends into the crags upon which it is built. It was here that two of the island's folk heroes, En Cabrit and En Brassa, defended the castle against the forces of King Alfonso of Aragon, eventually to be captured and put to death by burning.

Not very far away, and reached by a good road which crosses the Sierra de San Vicente north of Pollensa, the Castell del Rey stands on the cliff-edge above a spectacular drop to the deep sea. This Arab stronghold was rebuilt and refortified by Jaime I, to become one of the strongest on the island. As such it withstood a long siege by the Aragonese in 1285 in the reign of Jaime II, and was only surrendered by the loyal garrison in 1343 when finally it had to be acknowledged that all opposition to the mainland forces was hopeless. To put it in picturesque terms: it was here that the flag of the Majorcan kings flew for the last time. Its broken Gothic arches and ruined battlements in that lonely cut-off situation more than 1500 ft above the sea, is romantic in the extreme, and would have appealed to many a Victorian painter.

Turning to the opposite side of the island: the road from Artà to Cala Ratjada passes through Capdepera, which was one of the largest fortifications, with 400 yards of crenellated walls, four towers and one main gate. Soon after its construction early in the fourteenth century, King Sancho had built the little Gothic oratory of Our Lady of Good Hope inside its battlements. It is from hereabouts in 1232 that Jaime I, upon his return to Majorca, tricked the Moslems of Minorca into becoming his vassals. Though his resources were far from adequate, he despatched all the ships he had at his disposal to threaten the northern island. They numbered three galleys only, and could not possibly have prevailed had he not been inspired to light a long chain of fires upon the Majorcan headland, facing the channel, as though to suggest an insuperable force. The stratagem succeeded; the Moors capitulated.

The fortress of Cañamel, just to the side of another road from Artà to the east coast, is a little disappointing. Better perhaps to search out Santueri, further south, even though it is much harder to get to, at the end of what peters out into little more than a cart track. It is thought that the Romans may have had an outpost on this site in the hills which looks out over two coasts, as well as towards the island of Cabrera. Certainly it is among the oldest of the Majorcan castles. What can be traced of its foundations were laid by Jaime II at the end of the thirteenth century, and the whole defensive system was completed in a very short space of time, ready to withstand a sequence of sieges and raids in the Middle Ages. Charles of Navarre was held prisoner in the castle in 1459. The inland scene is lovely, hilly and well watered, a welcome relief from days spent on sunbaked beaches.

Those are the finest of the castles of the kings, from that period of the island's most illustrious history. The saints and the scholars came later. Most monasteries, cavalries and oratories are sited in high places, for reasons of symbolism and seclusion. The seventeenth-century Franciscan monastery above Randa, whose proper name is the Sanctuario de Nuestra Sēnora de Cura, is no exception, and makes a pleasant half-day trip from almost anywhere in the island.

Randa is midway between Alguida, on the road from Palma to Manacor, and Lluchmayor, further south. When approaching from Alguida, 22 kilometres from the capital, one first passes a turning to the left leading to the village of Castellitx and the ancient Hermitage de la Pau, which has an entrance in the Romano-Byzantine style. The second fork to the left leads almost immediately to the village of Randa, and then to a right turn for the ascent to the monastery. Though the almost conical, sugar-loaf mountain on which it stands rises to 548 metres above sea level, the gradients are well engineered, and driving is not difficult. On what is a recognised pilgrims' way there are two places of reverence to be passed—or visited: the Oratory of Nuestra Señora de Gracia under a huge rock and facing south where there is a simple hostelry, and another oratory dedicated to San Honorato. But the Franciscan monastery at the summit of the mountain is of course the main objective, for its own interest as well as for the supreme view overlooking as many as 32 villages of the central plain, and as far as Cabrera out to sea. In the spring, the spread of almond blossom seen from this height is something to remember.

Originally this was a simple hermitage, the chosen place of retirement of Ramon Llull, who though not yet canonized is perhaps the most venerated religious figure in the history of the island. We have already encountered him in his sacrilegious escapade in the Church of Santa Eulalia in Palma, again on the north-west coast, and in front of his sepulchre in the monastic Church of St Francis. He was born into a noble family round about 1235, and made himself notorious for his amatory excesses. Then, after his traumatic change of heart, he retreated to what for some time was to become his hermitage above Randa, and which grew into a school for Arabic studies where pupils were trained for work in the missionary field, but where he also found time to write his famous *Ars Magna,* one among about 250 books, most of which were written in the Catalan language. Under the patronage of Jaime II, and in any of his identities as grammarian, linguist, rhetorician, philosopher, mathematician, mystic, poet, chemist, theologian and even mariner he would have earned renown, yet he is chiefly remarkable as an apostle of the Faith, or, as he called himself, Attorney of the Gentiles. What sets him apart from contemporary medieval scholars and evangelists, many of whom were probably as accomplished and catholic in taste as himself, was his burning conviction that to be successful it was necessary to acquire a thorough understanding of the workings of the heathen mind. To this end he immersed himself in Arabic literature and all aspects of the Islamic faith, before setting forth on journeys which were to take him to North Africa and far beyond.

The Franciscans of the present monastery, which was founded on the site of Ramon Llull's original hermitage, are very hospitable, and are pleased to show visitors over both the old and modern parts of their religious house. They belong to the Third Order, so wear black habits instead of the more usual Franciscan brown. Many of them cross the Atlantic to join their brother house in the United States. The Library contains a great many valuable books, some of which are on display, and in the church there is a very beautiful fifteenth-century Madonna and Child, carved in sandstone and then painted; also a painted Crucifixion saved from a Dominican church in Palma, destroyed early in the nineteenth century.

Although so many hundreds of years separates the two figures, the names of Ramon Llull and Archduke Luis Salvador are inevitably linked through their connections with Miramar—where Llull founded his school for Arabic studies and Salvador built the first of many estates. He, too, was a scholar of many parts. His full name was Louis Salvator of Habsburg-Lorraine, and he was the third son of the last Duke of Tuscany, and as such cousin of the Austrian emperor. Luis Salvador first visited Majorca in 1847, when he was 20 years old, having made up his mind to turn his back upon life at the Austrian court, where he had had an unhappy love affair. Immediately a love affair with the Mediterranean became his ruling passion. Beginning with Miramar he acquired estate after estate, with the intention of preserving the amenities of a uniquely beautiful coast where he could live in style. He meanwhile embarked upon a real love affair with a local girl who, however, died of leprosy, leaving him once again broken-hearted though increasingly determined to channel his energies and considerable resources into all things Majorcan—folklore, language, arts and crafts, geology and natural history. He wrote more than 50 books on these subjects, 12 of which detailed the geography and topography of the island of his adoption. He spoke 12 languages, but wrote usually in German. During the course of his studies he acquired a particular respect for Ramon Llull, and not only edited a book to commemorate that scholar's 500th anniversary, but also dedicated a small chapel to his honour; and, in something of the traditional spirit, also provided a hostel where travellers might lodge for short periods; soap and fuel were issued free, but the travellers had to provide their own food and cook it for themselves—a practice which anticipated modern Youth Hostels. All in all, that Austrian aristocrat must be remembered for being a dedicated conservationist long before the term was coined.

Steep stairways bordered by cypresses and Stations of the Cross, form the typical approach to the heights on which most Majorcan oratories are perched. The Calvary overlooking Pollensa has 365 steps, and on Good Friday its entire length flickers with torches preceding the image of Christ down to the town's parish church. A road for cars snakes its way to the top, and that is the best route for people whose bodies and spirits would not stand the strain of all those heart-thumping steps. In either case the reward is great: the spread of the bays of Pollensa and Alcudia south of Cape Formentor, the jagged line of the mountain range which ends west of Palma, the more distant hills above Artà, the shimmering plain, pink with almond-blossom in spring, and, in days of exceptional visibility a glimpse of the entirely different conformation of the sister island of Minorca. Below, the tiled roofs of Pollensa look like something out of Toytown.

The hardier traveller exploring this neighbourhood, might care to attempt another ascent: to the Oratory of Nuestra Senora del Puig, on a hilltop 300 metres high, and three kilometres further along the road leading south from Pollensa. The small convent which sits on the summit may take about an hour to reach. The nuns who occupied it in 1371 were displaced in the sixteenth century, and their place was taken by hermits. In the present century the hermits turned monks moved to Monte Toro in the centre of Minorca, allowing the nuns to return to their own place. Their church has a fifteenth-century Catalan-Gothic altarpiece.

An easier vantage point to reach and one which is crowned by more impressive buildings, is close to the resorts of the east coast. The Sanctuary of San Salvador stands 500 metres above the Felanitx-Porto Colom road, and is reached by a good but exceedingly tortuous track from which there is a dizzying panorama in all directions. The medieval hermitage was enlarged in the seventeenth century, and now includes a hostelry and refectory for the public. In one of its chapels there is a specially fine Gothic reredos, and a carved stone Madonna, surrounded by candelabra, garlanded baroque capitals and other beautifully detailed ornamentation. Outside there is a giant statue of the Sacred Heart, in design not unlike a huge Albert Memorial, which overlooks the country of overlapping hills, scrub, vineyards and carob trees, while on a flanking hill there stands a huge Cross.

Petra could not be more different. The name may conjure up those splendid ruins in Jordan, but the two have little in common. It is a small town lying to the north of the

Palma-Manacor road, hidden away and unobtrusive, though in the Middle Ages it rivalled Sineu as a market town until its population was decimated by plague in 1651, from which it never recovered. It is a homely place, and could be insignificant were it not the birthplace of Fray Junipero Serra. His name is better known in the United States than in Britain.

Miguel Joseph Serra was born 24 November 1713 in the modest dwelling known locally as the C'al Bara in the Calle Caracar. After schooling in the town's Monastery of San Bernardino he was sent for further education to the Franciscan Monastery in Palma, where after graduation he adopted the religious name of Junipero, and as a companion of St Francis donned the habit of the order. Feeling a call to missionary work, in 1749 he embarked with others of similar intent on an English ship going to Malaga, and later set sail from Cadiz with 32 other volunteers for service in New Spain. An arduous voyage took him to Puerto Rico and Vera Cruz from where he travelled on foot to Mexico City; at this time the Spaniards were conquering the peninsula of Lower California, and the missionary role of the Jesuits was being taken over by Franciscans. The next step was to be the settlement of Upper California, by land and sea-borne expeditions. Junipero Serra set out, accompanied by 15 other missionaries, and it was largely due to this small nucleus of men that the spiritual conquest and peaceful annexation of California was achieved. Fray Junipero Serra founded the San Carlos Mission in Monterey less than a year after arrival in San Diego in 1769, and then embarked on a programme of establishing still further missions. One of the most famous, the Mission of San Luis Obispo, was built in 1772. Even though Indians thronged to the missions to be converted the policy of colonization seemed to be in danger of collapsing, and might well have done so, had not Fray Junipero journeyed back to Mexico City, where he pleaded with the newly appointed Viceroy of New Spain not to abandon the colonisation schemes which had at one time been aimed as far afield as Alaska. The result was that the missioner's pleas and his counsel prevailed, so that on 29 June 1776 the Colorado river was crossed, and what was to become the city of San Francisco was named in honour of the missionaries' patron saint, and enjoyed a founding ceremony that same autumn.

It is interesting to discover that the villages of Upper California and the cities which grew around them were named after the side chapels in Petra's seventeenth century monastery. Monterey, San Diego, San José and San Francisco are among them, and just as significantly, Nuestra Señora de Los Angelos y la Purisima—shortened of course to Los Angeles. The acknowledged 'founder of California' continued his missionary work, braving hardship, wars and attacks by savages until his death in 1784. He is buried in Monterey.

The house and small garden which was the Serra home is well kept and open to visitors. The simplicity of its construction and contents, restored to their eighteenth-century likeness, is most touching. The house (Calle de Caracar Alt No 6) was offered in 1932 to the City of San Francisco, which is now its legal owner. The annexe, housing a museum and cultural centre is in Majorcan style, and contains a great deal of material relevant to the missioner's life. As everything in this town is on a small scale, and close together, it is also easy to visit the Gothic church of San Pedro, which was founded in 1582 but not consecrated until 1730. It contains the font in which Fray Serra was baptised, and the pulpit from which he preached. The portrait in the sacristy was painted sometime after his death. A visit to the Monastery of San Bernardino, which was consecrated in 1672, will complete the pilgrimage, unless on the return journey to the main road, one feels the urge to visit the hilltop sanctuary of Bon Any, where a large stone cross celebrates the fact that it was here that Fray Junipero Serra preached his last sermon before embarking for the hazards and triumphs of New Spain. The ultimate step in the pilgrimage should by rights take one further: to the Hall of Fame on the Capitol in Washington DC where his statue has been erected.

7   The Other Shores

Cape Formentor is without doubt the island's most spectacular corner, and it has a luxury hotel to match, sheltered from the north and west and 13 kilometres short of the lighthouse which, from 209 metres above sea level, beams its light across open sea to three points of the compass, to be seen as far afield as Ciudadela, on the western edge of Minorca. Much of the beach below the hotel is reserved for residents, but part of it is public, with changing-cabins, palm-thatched umbrellas and other facilities for those who arrive by launch from across the bay, or by road from Pollensa and Alcudia to find clear water and sand, and a high degree of sophistication. The dramatic road to the lighthouse is particularly memorable even in a quarter famed for its confrontation between sea and cliff. The road, which has been put into good shape fairly recently, at one point tunnels through the mountain just before it reaches the little cove of Cala Muria where, incidentally coming as a surprise in a part of the island where the natural tends to dominate the man-made, there is a statue of one Mossen Miguel Costa y Llobera (1854-1922), the bard who expressed his poetry in the Catalan language, elevating it from the rustic form into which it is in danger of being debased.

History again begins to assert itself when the promontory is left behind. The ancient towns of Pollensa and Alcudia both possess Roman remains—nothing very impressive it is true, but worth locating because of their rarity. Pollensa, which we may already have surveyed from the heights of its Calvary, consists of terraces of brown houses laid out on a grid pattern which signifies that it was one of the inland towns founded by Jaime II. A good deal else has been preserved from early times, including a reputation for festivals, regional dances, peasant costume and local handicrafts, which include an attractive form of embroidery on canvas. The baroque barrel-vaulted church of Our Lady of the Angels, in the irregular plaza is lit by a single west window, and the similar vaults of the nearby conventual church of San Domingo are white-washed and have charming naif paintings on the walls, illustrating incidents in local religious history whose significance may perhaps be lost upon the outsider, but being none the less appealing for that.

The convent's cloister accommodates a school, hospital and old people's rest home run by the Sisters of Charity. One surprising feature to be found in the music school at the west end of the cloister is a bronze plaque honouring Philip Newman, the Yorkshireman who founded the town's annual music festival which is held on four consecutive Sundays in August. Newman died in 1966. Then, not forgetting the Romans, it is worth going down to the banks of the *torrente* below the Lluch road, to inspect from its own level the ancient stone bridge, which has one arch round and Roman, and the other shallower and possibly medieval.

Pollensa is one of the towns which for the usual strategic reasons was built a few miles inland, leaving its defence and maritime interests to be served by its watchdog, Puerto de Pollensa. This fishing village has an attractive seafront, with restaurants and cafés, and a colourful life which calls for the camera or the painter's canvas. But the beach is inclined to be narrow, and can be crowded in summer, bearing in mind that the distance from Palma by fast road is only 57 kilometres, an easy distance for an outing. To get more space for swimming or sun-bathing it might be a good idea to take to the water, by hiring a boat or taking a trip to some spot on the promontory which makes this one of the most sheltered parts of the island, or else to cross the bay to the coves south and west of Cape Formentor. Otherwise there are short inland trips, as for instance to the limestone caves of Campanet with their safe, well-lit passages threading their way around grotesque formations going deep into the mountain. The caves are only about four kilometres off the Palma road, just over two miles from the junction of the Alcudia and Pollensa roads, opposite a turning to La Puebla. The small and very old church of San Miguel is close to the entrance to the caves.

Alcudia sits astride the neck of the promontory which separates the Bay of Pollensa from the more open Bay of Alcudia. Confusingly the city, which earlier on was a Phoenician settlement, was called Pollentia in Roman times. Its present name derives from the Arabic *Al Kudia,* meaning 'the hill'. Medieval rather than Moorish defences proclaim this to have been a town of importance, though the gateways and flanking towers which catch the eye have rather an unreal, new look, due partly to excessive restoration. Though the bulk of the stonework was sold off by auction in 1871, two of the original gates have survived, while others have been reconstructed. One surviving bastion, built in the reign of Philip III has been incorporated into a sports arena. Most of these defences look out over Pollensa Bay. The maze of narrow streets in the inner town present many opportunities for photography. The principal street has houses which date from the sixteenth and seventeenth centuries, the period of the city's greatest prosperity. One looks for architectural detail: windows carved in Renaissance style, Gothic arched doorways, shady patios. This is a town for idle wandering on the shadowed side of small streets. Charlemagne is reputed to have lodged in the Calle de la Roca. There is also a first-class archaeological museum provided by American subscription, which contains funerary objects, coins and bronzes which have been excavated from the several prehistoric burial sites dotted around the edge of the bay, and there are also mosaics and sculptures of the Roman period.

When leaving Alcudia by the Jara Gate on its isolated site, and making towards Puerto de Alcudia, one comes upon the tiny chapel of Santa Ana, which is a perfect example of the very early Majorcan-Catalan-Gothic style such as was built immediately after the Reconquest. Then, a short distance along the same road, to the right, hidden away but well signposted, there is the charming Roman theatre, with its seating hewn out of the living rock. It was excavated by the American Bryant Foundation in 1953, and is thought to date from the first century B.C. It is the smallest of the 23 Roman theatres located in the Spanish provinces.

Puerto de Alcudia has separate harbours for streamers and pleasure craft, and a long waterfront. The bay curves in a wide arc south and then east, with low-lying country behind and very fine shelving sands. This is another high-developed area, in both senses of the word, and though people have room to spread out along the shore the hotel and apartment blocks have had to crowd themselves into a strip which becomes even narrower, where inland waterways have been created behind them as part of a land reclamation scheme aimed at draining a section of the Albufera marshes.

These wetlands, which in 1970 covered about 4000 acres, have a peculiar fascination, though they may manage to remain unknown to people staying within only a few miles of them. The reason may be that horizontal planes of vision, obscured by reeds some 8 ft. high, rule out the spectacular. But this means that they have secrets which repay investigation, as well as making a contrast to journeys over mountain roads. There are some lagoons, some canals edged by soggy tracks, rice fields, many windmills pumping water to a slightly higher level in the direction of Muro and La Puebla, where the soil is at its most fertile for growing vegetables, as well as resident water fowl of many kinds, and birds of passage and insect life galore. The hope is that this region will continue to be resistant to commercial interests, which have already succeeded in draining an area around the lake known (though not to conservationists) as Esperanza. Two *urbanizacions* have sprouted from the coastal strip: Ciudad Blanca and Ciudad de los Lagos. The threat to under-developed country persists in an island where revenue is paramount to other interests.

Whether or not the holiday visitor has leisure and perseverance enough to explore this unique part of the Mediterranean scene, he need not be ashamed of being lured back to the open shoreline, where further developments have been fitted in among sandhills and pinès, in what is aimed to be one of the best equipped of Majorca's playgrounds. Ca'n Picafort, once an isolated fishing hamlet, has an excellent beach for children a short distance to the south-east, but to the west in the neighbourhood of San Baulo swimmers should beware of currents. This part of the island has a very long history of settlement by overlapping civilisations: not only by the Romans and their successors, but by a prehistoric people, some of whom lived in caves, and others who were responsible for strange megalithic structures which neither time nor man has destroyed. The Phoenician necropolis of Son Real to the north of the coast road has been excavated, and its movable remains are in the Alcudia museum.

Very soon after Ca'n Picafort the road is unable to follow the coastline. The spur of the eastern mountain-range grows rugged where it meets the sea as an almost trackless hump on the horizon, except for the twisting road from Artà up to the Hermitage of Bellen, and a path, suitable for goats, leading to the summit of Atalaya de Morey, 432 metres above Cabo Farruch. The inland route passes the *talayot* of Sa Canova before joining the Manacor road below Artà, and continuing through Capdepera to Cala Ratjada. A feature of the country in these parts are dwarf palm trees of a type used for basket-making, hats and household and agricultural containers.

People who enjoy reading maps will notice that the east coast has a succession of *calas* or coves punctuated by headlands, which are marked as *puntas*. Many of these *calas* are narrow enough to be called creeks, as they are more like cracks in the land leading to sand and pebbles and deep water. A limited number have roads to them, and in any case the configuration of the land mass has put a coastal highway out of the question, so that each small place on the shore has to be dependent upon a minor branch off one of the inland routes. But wherever there are opportunities for getting wheeled traffic to the sea there are sure to be facilities for visitors, especially in what were until not very long ago no more than fishing villages, isolated from the rest of the island by a chain of hills and indifferent communications. The useful Firestone Map which can be bought in London as well as the Balearics indicates these natural harbours by a little boat steaming out to sea; the places simply named as *calas* are likely to be newer in terms of development or not built-up at all, according to their capacity for attracting custom.

Beginning from the north: Cala Ratjada, which is the furthest point in the island from Palma (80 kilometres) has been rather unimaginatively developed, but there are pines, mountain walks and good bathing at either Cala Guya, a short distance to the north on the other side of the headland, or at the Son Moll beach on the opposite side of the resort. For people who look for greater isolation, Cala Mesquida can be reached from Capdepera by 6 kilometres of mountain road. This is a holiday camp, and could be called a 'stay-put' place, as communications are not all that easy.

On the way south there is Costa de los Pinos which, as its name suggests is new, and has pines which bring shade and freshness even in hot weather, and also boasts about 250 yards of sandy beach. I have to say 'boasts' because many of the east coast beaches are pebbled. Costa de los Pinos is the nearest resort to Cañamel Castle, whose castellated shape dominates the valley, and above which a specially built road climbs high up on the headland, to arrive at the entrance to the Caves of Artà.

Because of its limestone structure, Majorca is famous for its caves, and the authorities were quick to realise their value as an attraction. The ones on the east coast are easily the grandest and the most accessible. Let no one imagine that a visit to the Artà Caves or those of El Drach and Hams near Porto Cristo will let them in for anything that approximates to the sport of pot-holing. Parties are conducted, and there is no danger, and little exertion except in the matter of walking some distance by flights of steps ranging up and down and round about through a series of caverns lit throughout by electricity. Floodlighting picks out special features, and balustrades have been put up wherever demanded for safety. The great surprise will be the temperature. The further one proceeds into the depths, the atmosphere becomes warmer and more humid instead of clammy and cold.

The Artà caves are reached by a flight of steps at the road's end, high above the sea. The parking and reception area give little idea of what is to come. Perhaps it would be as well not to go in for too much description of colour and formation, and just to say that some experts consider these caves to be among the finest in the world. The so-called Hall of Columns, for instance, is one where the fluted shapes of stalactites and stalagmites meet to make fluted pillars, one of which stands 22 metres high and is known as the 'Queen'. Piped Wagnerian music makes a fitting accompaniment to that part of the processional route which might well be the domain of the Nibelungen. At one point the rocks assume the shape of an enormous church organ, at another they seem to be growing into ferns and flowers, and in the largest cavern of all they look like a forest of swirling banners. The prescribed route from which no deviation is allowed, twists and turns cunningly, so that though it does not penetrate more than 310 metres into the hillside the impression is that it is much longer.

To return to bright sunlight and reality: two developments south of Costa de los Pinos run together and overlap—Cala Bona and the larger Cala Millor are bays whose chief assets are an extensive spread of beach, one nice thing being that for most of the way road traffic is kept behind the frontage line, which makes life carefree for parents and their children.

The atmosphere changes with Porto Cristo. In fact were it not for the coaches bent upon disgorging hundreds of thousands of visitors into the Caves of Drach and Hams, both of which are not far from the centre of the little port, this would be a restful place to stay, as in some Mediterranean Cornwall. There is sailing, even a little sand, and one may fish with some results from the quays. If not too successful, specimens of what might have been caught are on exhibition at the new Aquarium. Most of the coming and going is done by the cavers.

Something should also be said of these two bigger but not necessarily more beautiful cave complexes. Those whose name is translated as the Caves of the Dragon consist of four principal cavernous chambers: the Frenchman's Cave, the Black Cave, the White Cave, and Luis Salvador's Cave. Yes, the indefatigable Archduke has turned up again, pursuing his consuming interest in all things Majorcan. It was he who in 1896 commissioned Professor E. T. Martel, the famous French geologist of that time, to investigate and pronounce upon the caves. Martel and his Majorcan assistants discovered amongst other things that they contained lagoons of salt water which not only had a seasonal variation of depth caused by barometric pressure, but also an unaccountable but distinct rhythm.

Since Martel's day the caves have not only been made safe by the installation of concealed lighting, but visually more dramatic too, for an expert in public illumination was called in and briefed to floodlight all the important features, bearing in mind the variation of colour due to the presence of different minerals. He also made the best of reflections where these would repeat the columnar formations. It seems that the depth of the lagoons and pools can be reckoned by their colour: from blue through green to white—that is, from about 8 metres to less than 1 metre. The guides and the local guidebook will pinpoint phantasmagoric features which resemble animals, humans, vegetables, musical instruments including the inevitable church organ, but one of the most decorative is a ceiling formed of radiating stalactites, set like the prickles of a porcupine on the defensive. With only a little prompting, too, it is possible to conjure up whole pageants of classical figures and Gothic saints set in Byzantine architecture, with the colours of the formations varying from blueish-white to waxen, from yellow tones to red, and black where carbon is present.

The most striking feature is the Martel Lake, around which seating has been installed, to make an auditorium which can accommodate 3000 people. By the time the lake is reached members of conducted parties will probably be glad of a rest. What happens is that they are presented with a charming—almost magical—water pageant, in which musicians appear slowly and dramatically in illuminated boats to the tune of well-chosen classical music, not omitting of course, the *barcarolle. Son et Lumière* suit the romantic scene well, and when the performance is finished some few visitors are permitted to embark for a crossing of the lake, to mark the conclusion of the round tour.

It is a pity perhaps that a not dissimilar set of caves is situated so close that there is a temptation to visit both on the same day. The smaller Caves of Hams are at the top of the hill above Porto Cristo to the left of the Manacor road. They were discovered in 1905, and have seven principal chambers. The presence of calcium carbonate makes the stalactites and stalagmites white, while iron oxide gives a pinkish tinge. These formations, made by steady dripping, are said to grow from 1-3 cm. every 30 years. The lagoon here is smaller than that of Drach, but is of particular interest to naturalists because it contains strange aquatic insects, rather like centipedes. These are conveniently put on view in an illuminated tank. The various caverns have been given the inevitable fanciful names: Paradise Lost, the Madonna of Montserrat, the Cathedral, the Enchanted Villa, the Crib, the Angel's Dream. The name 'Hams' is explained, since it is a Mallorquin fishing term, and some of the stalactites, which rather strangely take on an upward turn, look just like fish-hooks.

There is another type of sightseeing to be done in this part of the island, something vastly different from Pluto's underworld. The Auto Safari Park has been set up a short distance off the road leading north from Porto Cristo. It contains a fairly representative collection of African fauna, in a setting which does its best to re-create a Disney-like Zululand. Lions are out of the question, but ostriches, flamingoes, peacocks, pelicans, elephants, hippos and rhinos and many types of deer may be seen from car or coach windows in a circuitous route. The majority of the animals seem to be more shy than wild, except for the apes who ingratiate themselves by perching on the roofs of cars and grabbing whatever food is handed to them.

The domain of sun and sea and all things Majorca is entered again south of Porto Cristo. The coast now consists of *calas* and *puntas* alternating more closely than ever before on a stretch known collectively as the Calas de Mallorca. Cala Murado is one of the easiest to get to. Then, after a stretch of roadless cliff one more indent reveals the traditional fishing village of Porto Colom, which has spread a little around its shallow harbour. This, incidentally, is the nearest resort to Felanitx and the eastern wine-growing districts, as well as the San Salvador sanctuary standing heavenly guard above them.

As might be guessed from its name, Cala d'Or or the Golden Bay, is newer. This really consists of several inlets fringed by rocks. The best of the beaches is Cala Gran, north of the resort, and Cala Llonga to the south, where there is anchorage for a limited number of small boats. Great care was taken when planning this resort: the new buildings are set firmly into the headlands, and do not rise above them; in fact they are more Ibizan in style than Majorcan.

A short distance further on to the south, but again only to be reached by making a detour, Porto Pedro retains quite a lot of its intrinsic identity as a fishing village, and therefore makes a good harbour for sailing enthusiasts. But for many people Cala Figuera is the most picturesque and satisfying port of them all. It has most of the ingredients of a good Majorcan recipe—harbour, pines, cliffs, boats for hire and all single modern amenities, though it must be admitted that the bathing is not of the best, and platforms have been anchored offshore so as to spread the swimmers out. Others may prefer to go a short distance to Cala Santañi and Cala Llombarts, further south. Between these two bays there is a photogenic rock called El Pontàs, the bridge. The inland town of Santañi is only five kilometres away, and makes an interesting place for pottering about, the colour of its stonework reminding one that it was from this quarter of the island that the golden stone of Palma Cathedral and a great many other medieval buildings was quarried.

As it is barren, the extreme south-east corner of the island has resisted development. The whole atmosphere of the coast now changes, though that is not to say that there are no pleasant places to visit between this point and the Bay of Palma. Colonia Sant Jordi and Puerto de Campos are not far from salt flats, on the opposite side of the road to a health hydro, and that neighbourhood is of special interest to naturalists because of its samphires, sedges, glasswort, sea asters and other salt-loving plants. Ornithologists also value it as a staging point for migratory birds, while rocky islets support colonies of the rare Audouin's gull, distinguishable from the herring gull by its black-banded crimson bill.

The island of Cabrera is about 17 kilometres out to sea, and Colonia Sant Jordi is a good place from which to recruit a fisherman familiar with the island's cliffs and contours. Otherwise, of course, there are the longer and more organized trips available by launch from Palma. Cabrera is just one hunk of rock, in no place more than seven kilometres across. The name of its highest point, Puig de la Guardia (172 m.) emphasises its importance among a chain of watchtowers which ring the coast. Because the island's water supply is inadequate, very few people live on it, except for the lighthouse keeper and a few fishermen and their families. There are no tourist facilities, not even a café, so that trippers should bring their own lunches. This is an island which has experienced a seemingly disproportionate amount of history for its size. This is due to its strategic position as much as its possession of an excellent anchorage facing the sheltered channel. It was sufficiently important in the seventh century to support its own bishop in a monastery. The fourteenth-century castle perched on a rock above the harbour was captured more than once by pirates, and was used as a convenient foothold for depredation of the main island. During the War of Independence, after the French had surrendered in 1809 at the battle of Bailén in Spain, 19,000 of their men at arms who had been taken prisoner were reduced to 14,000 by a forced march to Cadiz, where they were kept in hulks until their numbers had dwindled to 5500. They were then shipped to Cabrera, which became a sort of Devil's Island. Water was inadequate and provisions were rough and not at all ready. Though officers and non-commissioned officers were eventually removed to rather better conditions in Bellver Castle, and some even to England, the soldiers were kept on the island. Very few managed to escape, many died, and it is said that cannibalism was rife. It was not until 1814 that the survivors were taken off the island. A memorial to the dead was erected in 1849.

The Cova Azul—Blava in Mallorquin—justifying its name as a blue grotto which has been compared with Capri's—makes for rather more cheerful sightseeing. Deep water and white sand in combination create a strange blue light which reflects upward to the roof. The trip takes about half an hour by boat; there is no other way.

The south coast of Majorca is usually explored from the direction of Palma. There are several reasons why this stretch of coast is among the last to be developed, though La Rapita has a sandy beach, and Vallgonera a beautiful creek called Cala Pi. The comparative emptiness and aridity of this part of the island, and the fact that it lies south of every main road makes it virtually unknown country. But if a special reason is necessary for venturing in this direction, then let it be the Bronze Age settlement of Capicorp Vey, a few miles inland from Vallgonera, and also within easy reach of Lluchmayor on the Palma-Campos road.

Capicorp Vey (or Capocorp Vell) is important enough to be rated as a National Monument. It was brought to international notice by (who else?) the Hapsburg Archduke, though excavations did not begin in earnest until between 1918 and 1920. They revealed two square *talayots,* circular towers, dwellings, storehouses and possible burial chambers, all in massive drystone masonry, most of them aligned along what must have been an outer defensive wall. Most of the separate chambers have their own entrance enclosure, with pillars flanking an inner door. Some discoveries, including bronzes, votive objects, pins made of bone, and milling utensils have been transferred to the Archaeological Museum in Barcelona. The site is believed to have had people still living in it during the period of the Roman occupation of the island and it had certainly existed as early as 1000 B.C. The custodian lives in a farmhouse opposite the entrance, and can produce a pamphlet written in Spanish, French, German and English, giving maps and diagrams. Part of the fascination lies not only in archaeological mysteries which remain unsolved, such as are similarly attached to the *nuraghi* of Sardinia, but in Capicorp Vey's very existence in what must always have been an unproductive part of the island. Yet it is the poverty of the land upon which the settlement stands that has saved it from being levelled and its stones being carted away for re-use.

Between Cabo Blanco and Cala Brava, immediately south of the teeming resort of El Arenal and the end of the giant sweep of Palma Bay, the coast straightens out and runs almost due north and south, without significant indentations. Though not high in terms of the north-west, these cliffs are sheer, and there are few regular or even safe ways down to sea level. Part of the drive is through a military zone, where stopping is discouraged. What may be said for these first or last miles is that in almost every respect they differ from the other stretches of coast.

8   Minorca Today

The geography of Minorca could not be easier to grasp. One look at the map shows it to be shaped rather like a flattened kidney bean, that is, curving slightly from west to east, and without very striking ins and outs or contours. Nevertheless, investigation and a glance back to history will reveal that there are two exceptionally fine harbours at opposite ends of the island: Ciudadela in the west, the old capital of the island, and Mahon which supplanted it. Mahon is perched on cliffs at the head of a deep-water channel 5 kilometres in length and capable of sheltering an entire fleet—which indeed it did in Lord Nelson's day, though nowadays its importance is much diminished. Both cities have steamship connections with Majorca, and Mahon with Barcelona. Except in the south, most of the coast is a succession of *calas* and *puntas* in a miniature fretwork which would seem at first glance to be crying out for development, were they better equipped with roads. But more of this later.

The bare facts are that this second largest island in the Balearic group lies 43 kilometres from Majorca north of Artà, and 225 kilometres from Barcelona and the coast of Catalonia, with direct communications by sea and air, as well as non-stop flights from Britain. It measures only about 50 kilometres from east to west, and never more than 20–25 from north to south. This small land mass consists of an undulating limestone plateau bordered by cliffs, and has one central point, 357 metres Mount Toro, from the top of which the browns and greens of arable land and vivid green stretches of lucerne used for silage are spread out like a patchwork stitched together by stone walls. It is clear that these modest vital statistics give Minorca minimal shelter from Mediterranean winds, which can blow more severely and more consistently than is generally realised by people nurtured on the Riviera image. It is also significant that the northern districts are traditionally called the country of the Tramontana, after that wind which blows across the Gulf of Lyons carrying with it hints of alpine snows;

whereas the southern half of the island is known as the Mitjorn, from a dialect word meaning south wind.

It is this exposure to weather which has shortened Minorca's tourist season, so that the majority of hotels close for the winter. To balance this, the light breezes experienced at other seasons are far from being a disadvantage, and are welcomed by active holidaymakers and the sailing fraternity at other times. All in all, the pros outweigh the cons. Gluttons for statistics may like to know that, taking the year as a whole, the average temperature is 16.7°C, which can be broken down into an average mean maximum of 21.1°C and an average minimum of 12.2°C. The average rainfall is 40.2 in., from rain falling about 74 days in the years, mostly in winter but otherwise in showers which are quick to come and go.

This characteristic climate has so conditioned Minorca as to set its people and its products somewhat apart from those of its sister islands. No sub-tropical fruit, olives, almonds or citrus are grown or marketed, and a negligible amount of wine is produced. The land is almost entirely devoted to livestock farming; Friesian dairy cattle graze the fields, and to the knowledgeable their piebald patterns are a reminder that these are probably the descendants of pedigree animals imported by the British during their period of occupation. Sheep may be found on the higher and drier land, though they are not as numerous as they were in the Middle Ages, when Minorcan wool fetched high prices on the Mediterranean market.

In some other respects the pastoral scene is surprisingly English, though one misses tall trees. The pastures are inclined to be very small, made so by the presence of innumerable stone walls, in this case evocative of the West of Ireland, where stones and even boulders have been similarly gathered together as a measure of land clearance. The local limestone has been used since time immemorial for building, as is obvious in every corner of the island. In the rural context it appears in large farmsteads, whose groupings include barns and silos for the storage of crops, sheds for the housing of cattle, and a central rainwater cistern. Small country houses may be white-washed toy-like cubes; others circular structures harking back to the hundreds of prehistoric dwellings which are a feature of this island, and from which at first some of the utilitarian stone sheds are indistinguishable. The accent being on cattle, dairy products are of prime importance in the farming economy. In particular Mahonese cheese, which as well as being eaten fresh may also be dried and grated in the same way as Parmesan, is a valuable export.

Besides cheese, shoes and other leather goods, all of which may be found in local shops, jewellery and furniture feature high on the list of manufactures both for home consumption and export, and made individually by craftsmen, or in factories. These skills do much, these days, to keep a higher proportion of Minorcans at home instead of, as before, large numbers being forced to travel abroad—often to North Africa—in search of seasonal work or, hopefully, their fortunes, with the prospect of retirement after a well-earned homecoming. Islanders such as these do not make willing expatriates, unless by pressure of economic circumstances.

Of those who remain about half the population has gravitated to Mahon, the centre of things, around which are located most of the industries. Of course tourism has brought an increase in employment, but it is very noticeable to newcomers conditioned to other islands, that neither the Minorcan authorities nor the people they represent are prepared to stake all, in economic terms, or even in patterns of behaviour, upon this comparatively new development. Visitors are treated as welcome guests rather than as patrons, leaving the individualistic life of the island to proceed around them with little disturbance. Such an attitude is most welcome and admirable. The Minorcans are a clean and industrious people, totally without servility.

There is little fear of the indigenous culture being lost, or even prostituted. The traditional feast days are celebrated with great gusto, and without apparent concessions to tourists, just as they have been for centuries. These occasions are religious or historical, and sometimes a combination of both. For instance on 17 January Ciudadela celebrates jointly the Feast of St Anthony and the deliverance of the ancient city from the Moors by Alfonso III of Aragon in 1276.

Even more elaborate rituals are observed there on 24 June, which is the Feast of St John. That day in fact is the culmination of what can extend to a whole week of preparation for a programme in which the participants are the *caixers* or citizens of various degree, composed of the nobility, the clergy and the artisans, reinforced by the peasants, all dressed according to their rank. On the previous Sunday the crowds have assembled and have been greeted by the mayor of the city, who delivers to them a ceremonial banner which is then carried in pomp around the city, as an invitation to the fiesta—as if any reminder were needed. Events begin to move excitedly on St John's Eve, when official greetings or *caragols* are presented to the Mayor by troops of horsemen before they set out to visit the shrine of the saint. They circle the plaza three times, and all the while the band is playing a lively *jota* associated with *El Jaleo,* a word which may be translated as 'merrymaking on horseback'. The idea is for the barracking crowd so to upset the horses that they rear and cavort all over the place. The peak of horseback merriment comes with the chance of unseating the horsemen when they doff their headgear in salute to the Mayor on his balcony above their heads.

Music is an important part of the final day, too. In the afternoon the cavalcade makes its way once more to the Town Hall, in front of which the riders engage in an elaborate form of tilting known as the *juego de S'ensortilla.* In this hand-to-hand, horse-to-horse, man-to-man combat each *caixer* endeavours to protect himself with a *carota* or wooden shield against *rodiolas,* which are earthen missiles, apt to break easily and make rather a mess of their target. Another game which closely resembles medieval jousting is *el abrazo,* in which the contestants ride hell for leather at one another, lances poised. The merrymaking continues well into the evening, when those *caixers* who still survive and can canter around the streets are pelted with nuts. These are on sale everywhere, and make a crunchy surface on roads and paths. The finale is a midnight fireworks display in the Borne, which comes as a further reminder that the Feast of St John, as the longest day of the year, was celebrated by the ritual lighting of fires long before the advent of Christianity.

Mahon, the present day capital, is a good place to be during Holy Week, especially on Good Friday, when the Procession of the Holy Burial wends its way through the streets, watched by silent mourning crowds, the only sound coming from the clergy and their attendant choirs intoning the haunting funeral dirge known as the *Geu.* Later there is a parade of citizens wearing medieval costume. More joyously the Mahonese citizens celebrate the Feast of the Nativity of the Blessed Virgin on 8 September.

There are other special places to be on special days: Mercadal, in the centre of the island, for the feast of St Martin, which falls on 20 July is one. Richly caparisoned horsemen made a reappearance then in *El Jaleo.* A few days later there is similar equestrian pageantry at Villa Carlos, this time in honour of St James; and at Alayor, on 17 August, which is San Lorenzo's day, a special mass is sung for the *caixers* before parades begin; then on the first Sunday after 25 August the charming town of San Luis plays host.

Saints days with their attendant festivities come thick and fast during the peak holiday period. One of the most colourful celebrations during the peak holiday period. One of the most colourful celebrations takes place at Ferrerias, two-thirds of the way between Mahon and Ciudadela on 24 and 25 August, in honour of San Bartolomé. In *Sa Colcada* 14 horsemen wearing dress coats, white trousers and three-cornered hats ride in procession headed by a jester astride a donkey and playing eighteenth-century airs upon his flute. Mass is celebrated to the accompaniment of drums and fifes. Perfumed rosewater is distributed among the congregation, and later sprinkled over the crowds who assemble at the Town Hall for refreshment.

Most of these happenings hark back to the age of chivalry which followed the reconquest of Minorca, when Alfonso III granted estates to the Knights of the Order of St John of Jerusalem who had accompanied him. However, wherever we go we are constantly reminded that the island history stretches far back into still dimmer centuries. Minorca is well known to archaeologists as a place of strange prehistoric stone buildings, whose origins are still unknown despite numerous theories, none of which have come near to being universally accepted.

One of the most intriguing features of Minorca's prehistoric monuments, which are reputed to be among the oldest in Europe, is that there are more than 1000 scattered throughout the island. This seems to make little sense, because it argues a far larger population than the island could ever have supported at any one time. It has been observed that the island is an archaeological museum, open to the skies for all to see. The first inhabitants were cave-dwellers, who emerged during the Bronze Age to inhabit houses built of stone. Whatever was erected in those very early times tended to survive, because of the durability of limestone in its imperviousness to weather and the fact that no more perishable material was also employed in their construction. Even when buildings fell into ruin, stone was so plentiful that there was little likelihood that such huge blocks of masonry would need to be removed for re-use.

Nobody should leave Minorca without going a short distance out of their way to see at least one representative of each type of these strange buildings. There are three distinct forms: more than 50 *taulas* still stand. These consist of two megaliths; the upright one can reach to about 16 ft above the ground, and is firmly topped by a horizontal crosspiece itself some 13 ft long and five ft across, making a huge 'T'. One wonders what primitive technology enabled them to be hoisted into position—a problem akin to Stonehenge'. The assumption is that *taulas* had a religious significance, though their height seems to argue against their having been sacrifical alters. They are sometimes surrounded by a circle of standing stones. The second type of structures are called *talayots,* as in Majorca, where they are less numerous. These are round towers built of stone and of course without the use of mortar. They are higher than the *taulas,* and more complex. They taper from a circular base, which may be from 65 to 80 ft in diameter, until they reach an apex. Each contains a single chamber, but invariably without any clue to its function. Mausoleum? Temple? Ritual meeting-place? A chieftain's headquarters? Nobody knows.

Good examples of the *taula* and the *talayot* are present on a single site at Trepuco, just to the south of Mahon. These were excavated in 1931 by Dr Margaret Murray when she headed a team from Cambridge University. The third type is if anything even more strange. It is called a *nau* or a *naveta,* words meaning 'boat' suggested by their shape being that of an upturned primitive craft. The interior is usually divided into two chambers set one above the other. In this case the generally held theory is that they were communal graves, though no physical evidence has been forthcoming to substantiate this. One of the best preserved—in fact restored fairly recently by Professor Luis Pericot—is the Nau d'es Tudons, off the main road four kilometres to the east of Ciudadela. Both the sites mentioned are easy to get to; indeed they are within walking distance or an inexpensive taxi-ride from one or other of the principal towns. Some others are remote, because even in an island as small as this one whole districts are virtually roadless.

Thinking of the road system brings us back to more recent history. A single central highway runs like a backbone down the centre of the island, linking Mahon in the east to Ciudadela in the west. There is no coastal ring road, though offshoots from that central spine head north and south at intervals to reach small resorts and fishing villages where, in spite of recent development, care has been taken that new buildings will not conflict with the natural beauty. The central highway, the only road which can be dignified by that name, is in itself a memorial to the man who governed Minorca for one quarter of the period of British occupation. In the best tradition of colonialism Sir Richard Kane identified himself completely with the interests of the island. He is best remembered as the architect of this link between the superseded capital of Ciudadela and newer Mahon—an innovation for which the British were responsible. His forethought provided an artery through which the country's produce could circulate. At the same time Sir Richard was personally responsible for the introduction to the island of new breeds of cattle and varieties of crops, so as to raise the level of agricultural production. At the same time he mixed freely with the people he governed, and supported their interests whenever necessary, so that even now, so many years later, he is remembered with gratitude and even affection. A monument to his memory was put up rather belatedly in 1924 on the outskirts of Mahon and overlooking the first stretches of what is still known as Kane's road.

Another reminder of the (on the whole) beneficent British rule comes from a completely different quarter: Minorca is known for the manufacture of gin, which was specially introduced to cater for the tastes of the British garrison and visiting naval personnel. At the time of the occupation this spirit flavoured with the juniper berry had become popular with English people of all classes, and Minorca was not slow to take advantage of the fashion. The house of Beltran, which was founded in 1790, still produces the spirit according to an original recipe which remains a closely guarded secret. Their distillery on Mahon's waterfront is much visited by tourists during the course of a weekly tour of local industries. Beltran gin is about 60% proof, but the same firm makes 'Nelson' which, being a little stronger, may be more to the British palate. Both are very good. In more or less the same context 'Horatio' is a locally-made after-shave lotion, and 'Lady Hamilton' a toilet water.

The period of French colonialism does not lack its monuments either. Who has not heard of mayonnaise dressing? The legend is that this universal sauce was the brainchild of the Duc de Richelieu's chef, in an effort to make the sometimes crude island fare more palatable to his master. Minorcan food is more sophisticated these days, and kitchens make exemplary use of the best of produce grown and reared in the country. As usual in Mediterranean regions, the beef and the lamb may not compare favourably with English, but veal is plentiful because it is a by-product of the dairying industry. Fish and shellfish are popular, though the latter, even prawns, have taken on an inflated value due to their demand as hor d'oeuvres or *tapas* in Spain. Fresh tunny fish *(atun)*, red mullet *(salmonete)* and sole *(lenguado)* are plentiful, good and always come fresh to the table, while more and more visitors are beginning to overcome prejudice in appreciation of fried octopus *(pulpo)* and squid *(calamar)*. As for fruit and vegetables, these are grown in such variety that they need not be named. Apart from the Mahonese cheese, which those in the know eat neat with knife and fork, and the excellent processed cheese of the 'El Cesario' brand which comes in the usual foil-wrapped triangles, there is another Minorcan speciality to be indulged in happily—the locally made ice-cream, which far exceeds in creaminess, flavour and quality anything usually produced in England or on the continent. Connoisseurs rate it as superior to the Italian product. Most of it is made in Alayor, the first township on Sir Richard's road to Ciudadela.

9 Two Capitals and the Road between

The English were responsible for the transfer of the seat of government to Mahon during the longest of our three periods of occupation, which were from 1708–56, 1768–82 and 1798–1802. The move from Ciudadela took place in 1722. The decision was dictated not so much by internal administrative reasons or local politics but because Mahon's unique roadstead made it much more convenient for government to keep in close touch with the Navy, its garrisons and supply depots, by concentrating civil affairs conveniently and safely at the head of a deep-water channel almost five kilometres in length, narrow and easily defensible from cliffs on either side, and additionally protected by islands capable of fortification. The port of Mahon could accommodate and maintain an entire fleet, and had a reputation for impregnability. History does not absolutely bear out this claim, since it had been taken by Alfonso III, King of Aragon, in the late thirteenth century when freeing the island from the Moors, and the French also had invaded in 1756, though in that instance they had attacked the British from their undefended landward side, a tactic which definitely infringed the rules of cricket.

First use of Mahon as a port was made by sea-faring Phoenicians, Carthaginians and Arabs, later by rival European powers during the War of the Spanish Succession and the Seven Years War and the Peninsular War against Napoleon. But when the emphasis of European power politics shifted, and naval engagements in the Mediterranean became less frequent, Mahon's strategic importance declined, and the island was left with a port and back-up facilities far beyond the needs of what was essentially an agricultural island. Though a Spanish naval station is still in existence on one of the islands facing the town's quays, and British and United States ships of the fleet occasionally pay courtesy visits, Mahon's role in the defence of the Mediterranean has by now receded into something approaching folk history; this can be evoked by taking one of the most interesting and beautiful sightseeing trips around a harbour which it is possible to envisage.

These days, invaders in the guise of tourists are apt first to set foot on Minorca at the new airport to the south-west of Mahon. Again, as with Palma, this must be a matter for some regret, though the surprise of arrival can to some extent be simulated in that trip around the harbour and its approaches. The accent throughout is on defence, both natural and man-made. First there are the cliffs of this fiord-like channel and vantage points reinforced by four islands from which enemy attack could be sighted and opposed. An invading force would first of all be confronted by the northern cape known as La Mola, a natural strongpoint 256 ft above sea level, and once bristling with guns. Fort San Felipe stood on the opposite shore; it was built by Charles V in the sixteenth century, but was refitted by the British at a cost of 1½ million pounds two centuries later. It is now ruined. There is a connection by secret tunnel with Fort Marlborough, otherwise the Malborough Redoubt, above the Cala de San Esteban, which is in better repair, and where these days sightseeing launches usually put their passengers ashore. This entrance to the harbour was the scene of the Duc de Richelieu's successful blockade of Mahon in 1756, which was followed up by his troops' disembarkation at the opposite end of the island. It is said that the French avoided the more difficult landing, head-on confrontation and possible stalemate for no better reason than that they had found themselves without charts of Mahon harbour. In any case the defenders were taken by surprise. A naval relief squadron under Admiral Byng was immediately despatched to relieve the hard-pressed garrison, but as soon as he was intercepted by the enemy he sailed ignominiously away. He was to pay the price for cowardice by being courtmartialled and condemned to death by firing squad.

The islands become the focus of attention on the trip up-channel towards the present port of Mahon. The first, the *lazaretto* or New Quarantine Island is exactly what its name suggests. It was here that victims of the plague were housed. High walls were built around the island in the belief that these would prevent windborne infection from reaching the city. Even now this macabre island conveys a feeling of uneasiness to those visitors who had been successful in obtaining a permit to land. Applications should be made in good time to the Department of Sanitation. Visitors are rewarded not only by historical detail such as the lions, the Spanish seal and the flag of Spain sculptured over the entrance and brought from Fort San Felipe, but much more importantly the walls enclose one of the most curious chapels ever to be seen. It is circular, with a central altar, the pews being in the form of individual cells provided with grilles for the complete isolation of the unfortunate sufferers. Those who perished were buried in unmarked graves, because the scale of epidemics made positive identification too complicated to be undertaken. This island replaced the smaller Old Quarantine Island, the next to be reached. It was leased at the beginning of the nineteenth century to the Mediterranean squadron of the United States Navy, the forerunner of their present Sixth Fleet, and remained their headquarters for over a quarter of a century also becoming the training place for some midshipmen who where eventually to win fame as admirals during the American Civil War. The practice came to an end in 1845 with the founding of the U.S. Naval Academy at Annapolis.

The quarantine islands are overlooked from the left or port shore by Villa Carlos. When the French took Fort San Felipe they also overran British-built Philipstown, outside the redoubts, which had been planned as a satellite garrison town. But when Minorca was restored to the British at the end of the Seven Years' War the new Governor of the island, Sir James Murray, ordered the town to be levelled in case it should ever again serve as cover for enemy attack. Its functions were then assumed by Georgetown, newly built and named after George III, but which nowadays goes by the name of Villa Carlos. Understandably this is the most English and the most Georgian of Minorca's towns. Some of its houses still have fanlights over their doors, and iron knockers as well as, more remarkably, sash windows such as are rarely seen except in Britain. But the most striking memento of British naval and military power is the enormous barracks and parade ground in the centre of a town the whole of which has been planned with regimental precision. The barracks, reminiscent of Aldershot, are now occupied by units of the Spanish army. It is rumoured also that on occasion local folk dancers break out into their own version of the Highland Fling, complete with the wearing of the kilt, as a throwback to associations with the Black Watch.

The waterfront below the town has pleasant fishermen's bars converted from old boathouses, and quays overlooking the coming and going of yachts and local craft. This is a relaxed place in which to idle. It has hotels, one of which occupies the Georgian house of El Fonduco, the residence in Nelson's day of Admiral Lord Collingwood. He returned to Minorca after Trafalgar and the death of his friend, to continue as Commander-in-Chief Mediterranean for another 4½ years, but died at sea on leaving the island. Nelson is said to have lodged in another Georgian mansion on the opposite shore. Both admirals would have been within semaphore distance of one another. Golden Farm, or Villa San Antonio is privately owned and is beautifully kept, and still contains a great deal of valuable furniture and china. Incidentally the house is not golden, but colourwashed pink, but the gardens are luxuriant with flowers of all hues. Though not regularly open to the public, on occasion permission to view is granted to visitors with a particular interest.

At the turn of the eighteenth century Port Mahon was exceedingly busy, over 1000 ships using it annually. They took on water and victuals at Cala Figuera, below El Fonduco—nowadays known as Hotel del Almirante. At that time a freshwater stream had an outlet into the channel, and water could be stored in cisterns against eventualities. These days the storage tanks contain petroleum.

Further in, going by water still in the direction of Mahon which is only four kilometres from Villa Carlos, we reach another island, the Isla del Rey. It was here that Alfonso III landed in 1287. The military hoispital on the island was built by the British. Though in Spanish hands it is still operational, so to speak, and permission to visit may be obtained from the Military Commander at Port Mahon. Sailing on again we pass the Club Maritimo before reaching the inner harbour, commercial docks and the naval base, which has been built out on an artificial island, and has a typically Georgian clock tower. This approach to Mahon gives the best view of the city strung along at the top of the cliff so that the way up is either by a spectacular flight of steps, or by a zig-zag carriage road. The capital's three oldest churches add interest and a focal point to what is already a picturesque scene.

If for any reason it should prove impossible for the visitor to tour the harbour by launch, as it might be in off-season months, everything can be seen by road, using bus or car, and walking a little. Besides Golden Farm, there is one more relic of the colonial past on the opposite shore: the cemetery which was created at the beginning of the nineteenth century for the burial of non-Catholics. It is a small walled piece of ground above a cove. Amongst the graves, the majority of which are those of American seamen, is that of Nelson's faithful major-domo, Edward Gaynor Fry, who after the loss of his master at Trafalgar retired to Mahon and set up in business as a ship's chandler, and also played a prominent part in the small Quaker fraternity. It is not always possible to find the custodian so as to be admitted to the cemetery to read the inscriptions, but as it is on a slope a good deal can be seen from outside.

Mahon is a compact town, and sightseeing is easy, in fact no more than a pleasant walkabout with unlimited opportunities for sitting around, taking refreshment and observing life. The pressures on this island were light, and its capital did not attract much urban development. When the time came for growth, this was kept away from the walled town with its fourteenth-century fortifications, and was restricted to the suburbs, where there was more space. Few of the old defences still stands, and the one important survival of the early period is the small San Roque Gate, built in the reign of King Pedro IV of Aragon in the sixteenth-century Gothic style, with flanking quadrangular towers and a sundial in its western façade. Instead of creating an entry, it now almost blocks the street, and its chief importance is that it houses a small tourist information office. Another, busier office is to be found in the Plaza del Explanada, the town's largest square.

This perhaps is the place for a warning that though street names are displayed prominently enough to assist one to find the way around with a map, some individual public buildings give little clue as to their identity, and newcomers may have difficulty in locating such places as museums, or even the tourist offices. This may be partly a desire on the part of the authorities not to obtrude with too many direction signs, but the real reason could well be a healthy and proud take-it-or-leave-it attitude which comes as something of a relief on this highly individualistic and independent island.

Though Minorca experienced and suffered the same succession of conquests as others in the Balearic group, except for the megalithic remains and a few Greek and Roman relics in the museums, there is a scarcity of evidence of early civilisations. In fact it has been said that Mahon's history began—and ended—in the eighteenth century. The island failed to keep up with the rest of the Mediterranean during the Middle Ages, which elsewhere was a period of commercial growth. It remained provincial and inward-looking, the chief contact with the outside world being an obligation to shelter the king of Spain's ships and to victual them with local produce. However, impact was made by the constant attack of the Berber pirates of North Africa, against which the coastal *abbalayas* or watchtowers were an inadequate defence. Mahon was sacked in 1535 by the notorious piratical Barbarossa, just one year after Ciudadela had been ravaged by the fleet of the Ottoman emperor Selim II, shortly after it had run aground outside Fort

San Felipe.

Even the town's churches, lovely as they are, and with Gothic antecedents, were largely rebuilt in the eighteenth century. The church of Santa Maria, on an island site between the Plaza Conquista and the Plaza Generalissimo Franco, not far from the head of the stairway above the port, makes a good place to start. It was built in the thirteenth century after the reconquest of the island, but in 1772 was entirely reconstructed in the then fashionable neo-classic style of architecture. The interior is simple, with a single nave lit by arcaded windows at a high level. The building material is natural stone, which offsets the red marble altarpiece and two baroque side chapels. But the most important thing here is the monumental church organ built in over the west door which is something very special, even in a field of art which never, until the days of the cinema, went in for mass production. This particular instrument is the work of an Austrian, Johannes Kiburz. It was installed in 1810, after being brought all the way from Austria, at a period, be it noted, when the Napoleonic Wars were at their fiercest. The rules of warfare were in certain aspects more gentlemanly in those days, and as proof we can examine in the museum across the way the correspondence dealing with transport difficulties, conducted between the presiding bishop and no less a personage than Admiral Lord Collingwood. The result was the installation of a magnificent instrument with four keyboards, 51 registers, and as many as 30,000 pipes.

Upon leaving Santa Maria, it is likely that the visitor's attention will be captured by the archway on the other side of the square, because its masonry frames a view of the harbour, as though posing for a photograph. A statue of Alfonso III, cited as Alonso on its pedestal, is set up nearby in memory of his deliverance of the island. To the left when facing the harbour, and rather difficult to recognise unless you are specifically seeking it out, there is a grand Georgian building, more palace than house, complete with classical columns and pediments. The Casa de Cultura houses the Fine Arts Museum, archaeological collections, and extensive archives in a section of the public reference library. (Unfortunately in recent years this building was surveyed and found to be in a dangerous condition, so that at the time this book goes to press it is impossible to forecast when it will be re-opened.) The exhibits in rooms on the ground floor included Roman coins from the time when the town was called Portus Magonis; some Moorish decoration; Gothic statuary and Catalan ceramics—as well as Punic remains brought from Ibiza. The collections are supplemented by a variety of objects which have found their way here as bequests, including such exotic things as Mayan and Aztec artefacts. Of interest too is the small art gallery, which houses the portraits of King George III and Queen Charlotte, which once held pride of place in the Ayuntamiento or Town Hall.

This is the next port of call, because it is hard by and unmistakable as a civic building of some importance. The Town Hall, once called the Casa Consistorial, was begun in 1613 but entirely transformed in 1788. The arcaded façade with its wrought-iron balconies is additionally graced by a clock of English make which was installed by the beneficent Sir Richard Kane. It continues to keep good time. The pictures in the Ayuntamiento are more of interest as civic history than as works of art. At a lower level there is a small vaulted room containing examples of the whole range of saleable local crafts. They include fascinating model sailing ships which are a speciality of the town of San Luis.

Wandering off from here through the Plaza de España one reaches another good-looking church. The dome of the Church of Carmen contributes to the interesting skyline when seen from the approaches to the port. This church was built in 1751, and was the conventual church of the monastery of this name. The interior is huge, and its walls display a great many paintings of interest. The old monastery's cloisters are next door, and it may come as something of a shock, and then as a fascination, to find that they have been converted into the town's produce market. An abundance of fruit and vegetables are piled centrally in stalls, while the meat—which sometimes offends the sensibilities of northern Europeans who are no longer used to the sight of carcases in their butchers' shops—is discreetly tucked away in alcoves. The fish market with its tiled roof is a separate building, but no less colourful with its still-life displays of Mediterranean fish and succulent molluscs, in quantity and variety enough to whet the appetite for a quayside meal, either in Mahon or elsewhere along the coast.

We are still high on the rim of the harbour, overlooking the commercial docks and the waterfront, to the east of the Calle Abundancia or Avenida de la Victoria, which is the serpentine carriageway which traverses the flights of steps twice before reaching water level. The town behind consists of narrow tortuous streets, not at all Georgian, except for occasional sash windows, for which the rather comic word *winderes* has been coined. It is likely that inside many a house would be found furniture reflecting the fashion set by Chippendale, and faithfully copied by local cabinet makers. Small shops are the general rule, and shaded plazas well provided with pavement cafés and bars serve as meeting places. In particular the American Bar in the Plaza General Mola is a rendezvous for foreigners; it has been compared with Piccadilly Circus, even though it is not so devilishly beset by traffic. Otherwise there are several well-known bodegas, such as the Bodega Victoria in the Calle del Rosario, which maintain an old world atmosphere.

Wandering may take the stranger further east in the town, down the Calle Isabel II, where some imposing houses locally dignified as palaces have fine wrought-ironwork. One or two, such as the Palacio del Gobierno on the seaward side of the street, have entrances on to courtyards, but many of them give the impression of blindness, because their *jalousies* are kept shut as a precaution, impartially, against wind and sun. The Calle Isabel II will lead to the Church of San Francisco, with its great herringbone patterned west entrance, which is difficult to see in proper perspective because later buildings crowd in upon it. The conventual buildings on the landward side are no longer used as such. The interior of the church is in pinkish stone, surprisingly marbled, and with repetitive herringbone decoration on arches, and some faded and flaking frescoes. Perhaps the best thing about this church is its site on a terrace overlooking the upper reaches of Mahon's harbour.

Should there be time, there are at least two more interesting things to seek out. One is another museum, the Ateneo Cientifico or Science Museum, a description which is rather misleading when the accent is on natural history. It can be found, perhaps with difficulty, in the Calle de Conde de Cifuentes, tucked in behind the Plaza del Explanada. Stuffed birds, shells and even costumes are displayed, among other and lesser things, but the most important exhibits are seaweeds, said to be the most comprehensive collection of all the Mediterranean countries. There is also a library and a reading room. Everything is very intimate, the rooms are small, dark and rather fusty, and not at all what would be expected.

Some glamour lingers around the Teatro Principal, in the Calle Deya, despite its present use as a cinema. It was designed in 1824 by an Italian architect, the intention being that it was to be an opera house replacing the garrison theatre which was demolished after the retirement of British forces from the island. It served this purpose for over a century, in fact until the outbreak of the Spanish Civil War. Present day visitors who might feel disinclined to sit through a film performance solely in order to inspect the theatre, are usually able to contact the concierge at other times, so as to be ushered inside for a good look around. A tip will do the trick. Contemporary scores and playbills can be unearthed among the archives of the Casa de Cultura.

These are the places of most importance to be seen in Mahon, whether by design or accident during the course of leisured wanderings. And unless the stranger should happen to go around in circles, bemused by local concerns, no distances are great. The big Plaza del Explanada makes a useful point of orientation, especially as it is an open space and outside the labyrinth of the old quarter. One way of reaching it is by the Calle Cordona y Orfila, where there are banks and airways offices and similar useful addresses. One side of the plaza almost entirely consists of café-bars and restaurants; on another lurks the rather too well camouflaged Tourist Office, where information on the whole island may be obtained; and a third side is occupied by barracks. A war memorial in the form of an obelisk is striking enough, but the aesthetically-minded might prefer a dovecote fluttering with white doves, and the hungry will find sausage stalls. A few doors along the Calle José Maria Quadrana, leading from one corner of the plaza, we find the bus office. This is the place for checking timetables for every route, and it is also a departure point for some. It should be appreciated that in order to avoid the traffic congestion which would come from routing buses through the town, most of them have their own departure and starting points in convenient streets. For instance, though the Ciudadela bus arrives and departs from outside the main office, the one to Villa Carlos and San Luis and beyond use the San Roque square, at the other end of the town.

Sir Richard Kane's highway drives ahead to link Mahon with Ciudadela, taking in three market towns on its way. Except for Mount Toro, which can easily be sidestepped, there are no topographical obstacles. The land climbs almost imperceptibly on the outskirts of the city, to reach a height definite and flat enough to be called a plateau, which produces a clear view to either side. The best farming land spreads out to the north: arable fields yielding corn crops, beans, potatoes, clover and other feeding stuffs, variously green in spring, but apt to be parched later in the year. The south is more craggy and distinctly rougher, though everywhere there tend to be bare patches eroded by wind, alternating with sheltered, lush pockets of cultivation. The fields are divided by stone walls, in height, depth and frequency enough to daunt any follower of the Galway Blazers in the west of Ireland. There are not many field gates; farmers go from one field to another by making gaps, then rebuilding them. Stones dominate the landscape; often they are piled in conical structures so similar to prehistoric dwellings that the new and impromptu is sometimes almost indistinguishable from the old. However, at least one important *taula* should be noticed on this route: the Talati de Dalt, to the left about 5 kilometres from Mahon. Stones elsewhere make protective enclosures for individual trees, and for wells. The gem-like fields in their limestone frames are grazed by milch cows, toylike in their black and white patterns. The accent being on milk production there are not many bullocks or other beef cattle to be seen. Male calves are usually killed as veal before they have a chance to consume the precious milk which will have cheese as its principal end product. Many of the farmhouses have plain and shallow pedimented fronts, and preside over ranges of substantial buildings, perhaps colourwashed in basic terracotta, and handsome in their sturdy practicality.

Alayor comes first of the three market towns on this road. It is a quiet place of white houses in narrow streets, with a pink-tinged church dedicated to San Diego. The local name of the church is Sa Lluna. Its cloister recalls the primitive Californian missions founded by the Spaniards. No one would be likely to imagine, from the modesty of this small town, that its name appears in the address books of many a celebrity. This has come about because one of the inhabitants is a shoemaker of such excellence that he makes for the royal house of Monaco, and for other notabilities, according to their orders and measurements, as well as for more casual socialists who visit the island in their yachts. As a more recent development, and for everyday consumption, there is Alayor's famous ice-cream.

Mount Toro is now ahead and to the right. This being Minorca's one and only eminence it is easy to see, rearing above rocky outcrops, red earth, pines and pastures. A side road leads from Mercadal to the summit, so that if the ascent is made by car or taxi it might be a good plan to walk down, and to have greater leisure for the changing view from a zigzag track. The sisters of St Anthony and St Paul moved to this secluded spot from Nuestra Señora del Puig, near Pollensa in Majorca, when they vacated that hermitage for re-occupation by the nuns who had previously settled on that other ancient hilltop. The seventeenth-century conventual church here, dedicated to the Virgin of Mount Toro, has recently been restored. The hermits are hospitable, and refreshments are obtainable. As might be expected in such a dominating position, there are remains of an old defensive watchtower.

Mercadal, at the foot of the mountain 21 kilometres from mahon, owes its importance to its being at the very centre of the island and the junction of several roads leading in four directions. Neither Alayor nor Ferrerias are so equipped. Similar to Alayor, Mercadal has earned a name for itself in the shoemaking trade, though its products are more mass-produced. Particularly it is the home of the inventor and maker of *albarcas típicas Menorquinas,* which deserve to be brought to the notice of all visitors to beaches, cliff walks and stony archaeological sites. Though their name suggests some exotic breed of bird, these are quite simply soft cowhide shoes, rough on the outside, lined, and soled with rubber from car tyres which having fulfilled their function on the roads are now guaranteed for another 5000 miles afoot. They are cheap.

Further along the way, Ferrerias has a reputation for fertility: human fertility. The proof is that its streets are alive with healthy children. This little town of red and white buildings is mainly agricultural and geared to the disposal of farm produce; actually it was founded for this purpose by the early kings.

The Naveta d'es Tudons, off the main road to the left about four kilometres from Ciudadela, is clearly signposted. It cannot, and should not, be missed, since it is the most complete, as well as the most accessible of its strange kind. Two further prehistoric settlements can be reached from the Naveta d'es Tudons by turning back along a parallel minor road. Torrellafuda and Torretrencada are both marked on the Firestone map.

The first approaches to Ciudadela are marked by factory developments which appear to be indiscriminately dotted around, without apparent planning. But such criticism tends to be forgotten as soon as the town itself is reached. At very first sight Ciudadela proclaims its distinction. Gone is the British element, to be replaced by a Moorish look with overtones of French adding up, more logically than might be supposed, to something completely Minorcan. The Plaza Alfonso III, at the end of Kane's road, is vaguely Gallic, with a few pavement cafés, a kiosk, rather dusty trees and a central fountain. But foreign influences are dispelled after plunging ahead on foot into the darknesses of the old town. Paved streets run at all angles, the most intriguing of them lined with thick squat arches consisting of bulbous white-washed pillars and low vaulted roofs known as *voltes*. Small shops, deeply inset, sell colourful and precious objects.

It immediately becomes apparent that though Mahon is well established as the administrative capital, Ciudadela has never relinquished its dignity as ecclesiastical centre of the island. No better proof could exist than the cathedral in the Plaza de Pio XII, which, it almost goes without saying, was the site of a mosque at the time of the Reconquest. The Christian building was not completed until early in the fifteenth century. Since then it has been provided with a revamped façade and two side chapels, resulting in a neo-classical look superimposed on what was once pure Gothic. The sober interior has retained much of the older tradition, with a nave in the Catalan style and a doorway known as the Puerta de Luz which has carved mythical animals bearing the coats of arms of Ciudadela and the kingdom of Aragon. There are five narrow windows at the east end, and the choir stalls have representations of individual saints painted behind them. A clock on the south side of the nave brings us back to the present century, with an inscription proclaiming it to have been made in 1946.

The Episcopal Palace is immediately alongside the Cathedral, and one of its side entrances is furnished with a lovely old brass knocker. From here it is only a few steps into the Plaza Generalissimo, which is more familiarly known as the Plaza del Borne, and where there is an obelisk erected in honour of the valiant resistance of the city's people against invasion by the North African Moors in the year 1588. This is the part of the town to which everyone instinctively gravitates, one excellent reason being that on the right there are remains of old fortifications from whose parapet there is a view of the navigable waters which brought Ciudadela its importance, and still do. The quays below serve not only coasters and the inter-island steamers which ply to Alcudia and Palma, but also provide berths and moorings for yachtsmen to a degree of excellence which justifies a rating in the prestigious Blue Book of the Yacht Club of Monaco—the sailing fraternity's Debrett. All navigators who have reached this haven will have firmly fixed in their memories the medieval tower of Saint Nicholas, now out of sight, at the entrance to these waters.

But for the landbound there is another reminder of the Middle Ages in the Governor's Palace in the Borne. It was once the Alcazar or palace of the Moorish rulers of the island. Nowadays, after restoration in the nineteenth century the building functions as the Ayuntamiento. Because it contains working civic offices its rooms may only be viewed after office hours, that is in the afternoon between 6 and 8 pm, and on Saturday between 12 noon and 1 pm. It is worth planning sightseeing so as to fit in with these hours. The town hall contains a splendid Gothic reception hall with panelled ceiling and imposing wrought-iron lamps, and there is a museum which contains amongst other things the banner carried by Alfonso of Catalonia and Aragon—to give him his double title—when he landed in 1287 and set to work to oust the Moors. There are also paintings of the town's most notable citizens of all periods and, keeping them company a portrait of George III which somehow got left behind in the British removal. Another portrait of interest to outsiders is that of David Ferragut, the first admiral of the United States Navy, who became an honorary citizen of Ciudadela. This is the birthplace of his father, Jorge Farragut Mesquida, who at the age of 17 emigrated to seek his fortune and eventually enlisted in the U.S. army, then in the navy, into which he was followed by his son. Behind the gilded and roseate stucco of the palace of the Marqués de Menas Albas, in the Calle San Sebastien, there is preserved with some formality the bedroom containing the actual bed in which the admiral slept when he paid a visit to his father's home town in 1867.

The palaces or glorified town houses of Ciudadela are a definite feature of the place. Their eighteenth-century appearance, not at all Georgian but echoing the taste of the Renaissance, proclaims them to be buildings of consequence. Some are still in the possession of members of the Spanish aristocracy who for political reasons had to flee from the mainland and were only too glad to be able to settle peaceably in Minorca. One or two, such as the Torresaura Palace which is owned by the count of that name, have archways leading into spacious courtyards. The Salort Palace, also in the Borne, and the Palacio de Martorell and Casa de Vigo are others. There are churches, too, but with the possible exception of the church of San Francisco and its seminary, none of them are of particular importance when set against the cathedral. Some are shabby, and have declined into secular use. The arcaded streets with their boutiques, the little shops selling handmade luxury goods are more rewarding, making this a happy hunting ground at all times, but most festive of all during the St John's Eve junketings. Though there are *hostals* in the town, the better class hotels are situated on the Paseo Maritimo beyond the mouth of the harbour, and of course at the little seaside places within convenient reach by car, bus or taxi.

10   The Coasts

Minorca's basic road system makes it convenient to think of the scattered resorts and fishing villages in relation to Mahon and Ciudadela and the three markets towns on the island's spine. On the other hand perhaps this is illogical, because few visitors actually stay in the town centres, and still fewer inland. They settle themselves instead on the coast, either north or south in some place of their choosing, from which any trip inland must lead inevitably back to Kane's Road in quest of branches leading in other directions. These trips are often an important part of the holiday, because there is not very much in the way of organized amusements, except those which are provided liberally by sun, sea and cliff.

The brochures proclaim that there 120 beaches, and this may well be so. But it is one of the charms of this island that a very large number are inaccessible except by cliff paths highly suitable for goats, and in districts unmarked by roads. Nevertheless would-be explorers need not be daunted: the majority of those hidden beaches may be reached by sea from somewhere not too far away, and the local boatmen are reliable in picking up their Crusoes at prearranged times. And of course there is no danger of being cut off by incoming tides.

The south coast has attracted more development than the north in the form of *urbanizacions,* a word which is less doom-laden here than elsewhere, since a great deal of care has been taken to keep buildings low and to make the best use of contours and pine trees to prevent their becoming an eyesore. In this way the natural character of the shoreline is preserved, a policy which is helped by the fact that inlets hemmed in by cliffs and tumbled rock have deterred the road builders from lateral spread.

The corner of the island immediately south of Mahon has inevitably attracted its quota of development. Most of the seaside places hereabouts are within easy reach of San Luis, which is a charming town founded by the Duc de Richelieu for the accommodation of his Breton sailors, and as such as the

Gallic counterpart of eighteenth-century Georgetown, alias Villa Carlos. The town, known familiarly as *la ciudad blanca* because of its white houses which on their street side may have no windows at all, recalls its French phase with its church displaying the *fleur de lys* in its façade. Modern generations of visitors may be more appreciative of the fact that there is nightlife of a more varied pattern than that offered by the discotheques and ballrooms of the hotels. So there is always a certain amount of coming and going between San Luis and Mahon, and from the smaller neighbourhood places.

A succession of holiday resorts are grouped around San Luis, and stretch out from the harbour's entrance far along the coast on either side. Taking those to the south and west at random, Cala Alcaufar is a picturesque village until recently inhabited only by fishermen and a few Mahonese owning summer villas. These days many of the fishermen's cottages, which are customarily built over or alongside boathouses with individual slipways, have been converted to make additional waterside accommodation. They face rocks and rather shallow water, so that better swimming is to be found at the nearby new resort of S'Algar. Punta Prima, at the corner of the island and 12 kilometres from Mahon, has rather less character, and is apt to be noisy at weekends because it is a favourite with the townspeople of Mahon, besides having fine sand especially suitable for children and family parties.

Binibeca is further along the coast. It is picturesque in the extreme, and so it should be, because it is a working model designed to reproduce with some exactitude a traditional fishing settlement. The quays, the *voltes,* ironwork, paved walks, the houses which are white-washed roofs and all, and many with outside staircases, convey a glamorised but sufficiently authentic Hispano-Moorish atmosphere to make this a show place, and one with a convenient beach and good restaurants and bars, where very happy holidays can be spent.

Cala'n Porter, further west, has different but no less agreeable attractions. The best way of reaching it is through the small town of San Clemente near the airport. It is situated at the entrance to a very pretty creek flanked by well-wooded cliffs, typical of the south coast. One excitement additional to its good beach, exists in the form of caves, once inhabited by troglodytes. There are more than 40 of these prehistoric dwellings. The nearest, the Cova d'en Xoroi, has been converted to make a swinging and uniquely dramatic discotheque whose entrance is high above the sea. The series of other fiord-like inlets, known as the Calas Covas, with their caves, may either be reached from the San Clemente road, or in more leisurely fashion by boat. An *urbanizacion* a short distance inland from the principal creek is remarkable for the choice of its name: San Vitamine del Mar.

As far as access is concerned, all these places and many more are Mahon's. Further west Alayor becomes the key, especially to the Playas de Son Bou. One way to the smaller resort of San Lorenzo goes close to the Torre d'en Gaumés, a complex of megalithic structures which includes a *taula*, three *talayots* and several cave dwellings. Then just to the west of the Son Bou beaches, at the foot of the cliffs and within easy walking distance, we come upon one of the island's rare early Christian ruins: a fifth-century basilica with a ground plan showing it to have had three naves measuring 25×15 metres, each provided with an apse. A baptismal font in the form of a clover-leaf is cut out of one huge piece of stone. This church of San Jaime Mediterranée was discovered as recently as 1951.

As far as access to the south coast is concerned, Mercadal comes into its own because one of its roads leads through very pretty country, past the inland village of San Cristobal, which is famous for its enthusiastic folk-dancing. This road ends at the resorts of Santo Tomás and San Adeodato, which make full use of some seven kilometres of beach, delightfully compartmented by promontories.

Once again there is no coast road leading west from here. The creeks get narrower and deeper, until they are dignified by the name of *barranco,* meaning a ravine or gorge. The Barranco de Algender is the finest. It may be followed on foot the whole way from Ferrerias on its course parallel to the road, to Cala de Santa Galdana. This horseshoe-shaped beach is generally considered to be one of the finest on the island. As such it has inevitably attracted development, but one saving grace is that its cream-coloured cliffs, and most of the surrounding land, rise higher than the hotels, while many villas are hidden away among pines. This bay has the distinction of possessing an excellent four-star hotel. A secondary road connects Cala de Santa Galdana with Ciudadela, passing the Naveta d'es Tudons a short distance east of the city.

Ciudadela has its satellites on the coast to the south. These perhaps suffer slightly by being within such easy reach of the town, though this also has its advantages. In any event in terms of the Spanish mainland or Majorca these resorts are uncrowded and unsophisticated. The *urbanizacions* of Son Oleo, Cala de Santandria and Cala Blanca consist mainly of villas; other accommodation is limited. The beaches attract day visitors. Further on, around the south-west corner of the island beyond Cabo Dartruch, and reached by minor roads, the sandy bays of Playa Bosch, Playa Son Saura and Cala Turqueta, each with a backing of rocks and pine trees, are more relaxed.

The coast north of Ciudadela has been developed to take advantage of views across the entrance to the harbour, but from Cala Blanes onward the pattern changes. *Puntas* and *covas* are marked on the map but they are likely to be inaccessible, though the clifftops make good walking, as for instance to the Bajoli lighthouse, along a track good enough for cars, and from which one gets a happy sense of being on the edge of the world. By the time the coast has turned to run from west to east roads are scarce, except to Cala Morel, a small hidden place where the deep water is exceptionally clear, and, further on, Algaierens, which is bigger but just as isolated.

Mercadal then resumes its function as a 'jumping-off' place, first by minor roads to Cala Pregonda and past the salt marshes of Casa Novas to Binimel la Playa, and then for the scenic drive to the tip of the narrow headland of Cabo de Caballeria, east of Cala Ferragut. A better road to the east leads to Fornells, which many people consider to be the most attractive fishing village of all, with its reputation for seafood and opportunities for taking boating trips across the mouth of the deep-set bay, and for visiting the numerous islands in this natural harbour where fishing is the main occupation.

Fornells is better equipped with alternative roads than most other similar places. Not only is it eight kilometres by the direct road from Mercadal, but an alternative is offered by a lateral road to Mahon which avoids geographical hazards such as the Albufera marshes by keeping always a few kilometres inland. This road however is in close touch with places where there is a choice of accommodation for the holiday visitor, such as the Arenal del Castell, with pines and semicircular beach curving for two miles, Addaya and its tiny port and offshore islands and, further south, Es Grao on the seaward edge of the Albufera. At this last one choices of occupation lie between expeditions by boat to the interesting Isla Colom, walks through Albufera to observe the birds and other wildlife, the use of a good beach. Perhaps the island will have the greatest appeal, not only because it has two excellent and lonely beaches of its own, but also because there are remains of copper mines worked by the British in the eighteenth century.

Though it can never be done as a circuit, this survey of the island could end with a look at Cala Mesquida, which is one of the nearest seaside places north and west of the capital. The distance is eight kilometres and makes a good escape from whatever urban pressures Mahon may exert on her citizens who, however, give the impression of being contented as well as industrious.

11 Ibiza Then and Now

Unlike its sister islands, Ibiza appears to have slumbered for long periods without much in the way of historical happenings. This is in character with such an easy-going place. Colonization of the island by the Carthaginians began in 480 B.C., and it then became a model of civic orderliness as a link with trading posts on the Spanish coast. Furthermore it acquired a reputation which even now contributes greatly to what can be explored on odd sites and in museums; it was observed that there were no deadly animals or insects, and no toxic substances in the soil. This made the island an ideal place for burial, so much so that bodies, dead and dying, were brought in from far and wide for interment. This can be seen in the great number of burial grounds and Punic sanctuaries, far in excess of the estimated population of those times, which have been identified and excavated. The results are to be seen in the internationally renowned Puig des Molins Museum, which is close to the entrance to a Punic necropolis in the town of Ibiza.

When the Romans forced their way into the ascendant on the European and North African scenes, Ibiza was spared the humiliation of conquest by being admitted as an ally of the Empire. What was then the island of Ebusus thereafter remained subject to Rome for six centuries, continuing to be loyal to Julius Caesar at the time of Pompey's revolt. However it was not possible to escape the onrush of the Vandals in the third century after their conquest of Andalusia, nor capture by Belisarius in 535 and two centuries under the rule of Byzantium. The Arabs became the dominating power from the early eighth century, though they were constantly attacked by the Christians. In fact Charlemagne took the island in 798, and held it for three years. Though it had to be relinquished it was retaken in 813 and incorporated for a further period in the Frankish empire—after which the Arabs returned and ruled for 500 years in all.

Following the reconquest of Majorca, plans for taking Ibiza and Formentera were drawn up in 1234. A document of intent assigning the task jointly to the Archbishop Elect of Tarragona, the Infante Don Pedro of Portugal and the Count of Roussillon are among the most precious of the Cathedral's archives. The crusading fleet sailed from Barcelona in 1235, and the attack centred around the triple defences of the citadel. When the day was won and the time for division of the land arrived, the Portuguese prince donated his share—which was to have consisted of Santa Eulalia and surrounding districts in the north-east—to the King of Majorca.

Towards the end of the fourteenth century, following a dormant period, there were no more than 500 families on the island, while Formentera was completely depopulated. Activities were narrowed down to local defence measures against Moorish raids by means of watchtowers, and emphasis was placed on the ultimate safety of the Citadel. In contrast to the inhabitants of Majorca and Minorca, the Ibizan peasants doubled up as fishermen, mainly for purposes of survival, though in the eighteenth century, due to population expansion which taxed the island's resources, many Ibizans were recruited to crew privateers and subsequently earned heroic reputations, harrying both Berber and English shipping on the high seas.

The picture emerges of a highly individualistic island having little important traffic with the outside world in direct commerce and despite its proximity to one of the most vital Mediterranean sea lanes. In the past principal exports had been wood and charcoal to North Africa, but another natural resource of paramount importance was salt; the lagoons in the extreme south of the island, close to where the airport came to be laid out, had been famous from very early times for red salt which could be conveniently shipped from the quays of Ibiza town. Even so, it was not the Ibizans themselves who developed the trade but the Italians, who stepped in with their genius for commerce and organized its production and distribution to Northern Italy and many Mediterranean ports. For the most part the Ibizans worked as labourers alongside slaves and prisoners of war. When the salt workings claimed an undue number of the peasant population, so that agriculture flagged, foreign ships were forced to bring in cargoes of wheat on their incoming journeys. For many years ships made a practice of calling at Ibiza for the salt, which was used to preserve the fish in their holds, notably the cod and herring which were a staple part of winter diet in northern countries. It followed that from earliest times Ibizans were accustomed to the company of men from other lands, and this has been advanced as a reason for their accepting their role as hosts to an influx of tourists without loss of equanimity or good humour.

In point of fact, tourism only began to develop towards its present dimensions in the early 1960s; before that date there was little accommodation available, few cars, and no airport.

Ibiza and Formentera are grouped into an archipelago in their own right, well removed from Majorca by a seven-hour crossing by steamer from Palma, or a short flight. The largest satellite islands of Espalmador, Tagomayor, Conejera, Penyats and Vedra either form part of a submerged causeway between the two largest islands, or are more rocky, and situated off the west coast. It is possible to make arrangements to land on them, though they are too small to be exploited or inhabited. So much the better. Ibiza measures about 40 kilometres across, and no more than 572 square kilometres, ringed by about 172 kilometres of coastline made up of cliffs and rocky coves. All roads radiate from the town of Ibiza in the south, and though this old town is the star attraction on account of its antique beauty, it has few hotels and none at all in the highest grades, so that visitors prefer to stay at Cala Talamanca to the east or Playa de Ses Figueretas, west of the town. But the most populous tourist resort is San Antonio Abad, 16 kilometres away on the opposite coast, where its opportunities for spread have attracted the entertainments and tourist developments which many of the smaller coastal places have been spared.

The temptation is to regard Ibiza as mountainous, but hilly is a better description, as its highest point, the Atalayasa of San José, is only 475 metres high. This particular range is in fact the connecting link between the sierras of the mainland and the peaks of Majorca's north-west coast. The country in its natural state is typically Mediterranean, closely covered with pines, heaths and juniper scrub, though wherever the terrain allows it has been cleared to form areas of intensive cultivation for the production of vegetables, fruit and cereals, and there are flowers everywhere.

One of the most noticeable features is the oddly oriental aspect of the place and its people. (One may remember that North Africa is only 212·4 kilometres away, and the Iberian peninsula, which for so many centuries was subject to Moorish influences, only 83·6.) Many of the houses are built as cubes, and they can be extended by adding others, as though from a set of child's blocks. The majority are washed white with a thick lime mixture known as *cal,* and this acts as insulation against heat; but a few are blue, which is Moorish magic for warding off the Evil Eye. Windows tend to be narrow slits, and very few, while the roofs are usually flat, or on shallow planes of terracotta tiles constructed for the purpose of catching every drop of the rainwater which is probably an all-important factor in the family's domestic economy. Grander and more complicated systems of water conservation and irrigation have been inherited from the Arabs, who were masters of those techniques. They are still employed in the horticultural district of Ses Feixes, a short distance west of the town.

Berber influences can also be seen to be reflected in the islanders' native dress. Though many country people wear adaptations of traditional costume when going about their everyday life—such as voluminous black skirts, coloured kerchiefs and great, shady straw hats—these are no more than an approximation of what used to be. These days the full ceremonial dress of the people is unlikely be be seen except as part of folk-dancing displays, and in feastday celebrations, and sometimes country weddings. The women's costume consists of the *gonella*, a long black pleated tunic over which is worn a bodice with detachable sleeves and a double row of gold or silver buttons, and an apron below. Shawls are usually black, red or yellow, and the *cambuix* or printed kerchief worn on the head can be topped by a wideawake hat. Sometimes this headsquare is of white lace. For very best the *mantellina* or white shawl was *de rigueur*, combined with—strangest of all—the *abrigai*—a small red cape carried over one arm, like that of a *matador*. Sandals were usually made of esparto grass woven in openwork patterns. The finishing touch to this flamboyance is the *emprendada,* the massive and ornate necklaces of silver, coral or mother of pearl, or all three, and in earlier days gold. From these there may hang a double-sided locket containing the likeness of a saint—usually the women's name-saint, or the patron saint of the village from which she comes. In contrast to all this finery, the style of hair-dressing is simple; it is brushed straight back from the forehead, parted in the centre, and then plaited, reappearing often below the waist and tied with a bow with streamers to accentuate its length. Girls who are engaged to be married wear rings on all their fingers, and some of these have charms attached, a key and a heart having special significance in the circumstances. Though the wearing of these antique and unwieldy clothes has died out except on unusual occasions, some young women like to wear a modification on special days, consisting of a white dress with a stiff starched skirt held out by a series of petticoats, and usually a yellow head-scarf.

As for the men, their ceremonial dress is almost as striking: they wear black worsted trousers in winter, or white linen in summer. These are baggy and pleated at the waist, though they narrow before they have reached the ankles. A red or black cummerbund is wound around the waist, and in the folds there is stowed a knife. The white-sleeved shirt has a high collar, but this is covered by a silk neckcloth. The black waistcoat, very dandyish, is sometimes embroidered but invariably has a double row of silver buttons. The cap has a revolutionary or buccaneer air, because of its bright scarlet, and the way it juts forward jauntily from a black headband, giving the impression of a cock's comb.

The barnyard theme re-appears in country dances, especially in the courtship dance, in which the man struts amorously around his bashful lady to the clack of giant castanets. This dance is in two formal movements: the *curta,* in which the man leaps around her while she moves slowly, eyes downcast, in figures of eight. This develops into the *llarga,* in quicker tempo, when the stylised movements become more exaggerated. She pretends to be trying to elude his advances, until the pursuit ends in his towering over his now yielding quarry, before sinking to one knee. Another dance, the *dotze rodades,* to be translated literally as 'twelve turns', is only for weddings, and performed initially by the bride and groom alone, until they are joined by two bridesmaids, who though he confronts them, the groom must be careful to ignore. Sometimes at weddings the parents and grandparents of the couple lead off the *curta* for three circuits before the rest of the party joins in.

Music is supplied by three traditional instruments. The *flauta,* a flute made of oleander wood and usually heavily inlaid with metal, has three stops, and uses the diatonic scale. It is held in the left hand, and from the same arm the *tambor* or decorated drum is suspended by a cord. The single drumstick is held in the right hand. Another performer plays the *castanyoles,* the huge castanets made of juniper wood which measure about 15 centimetres. A fourth instrument, the *espasi,* should strictly be used only for Christmas songs. There is no written music, indeed the performers may be illiterate in a total sense, and their songs, known as *cantades* (or *xacotes* in Ibizenc) often take the form of burlesque and are bawdy, whereas the *porfedi* or battle hymns which are nearly as popular, tend to be serious and even inflammatory.

Besides Holy Week, All Saints' Day, and the Feast of Corpus Christi, to which great reverence is attached, the various saints' days of which there are many, are also times for merrymaking, which usually follows the processions and the churchgoing. As most of the Ibizan towns and villages derive their names from the patron saints after whom their churches are named, these feast days are easy to pinpoint. Often there is something special, as for instance the blessing of animals on St Anthony's Day at San Antonio Abad and midsummer bonfires at San Juan Bautista on St John's Eve. On 16 July, the Feast of the Virgen del Carmen, the celebrations are linked with the sea, since this is special day for seamen and fishermen, so that at the port of Ibiza and San Antonio Abad there are waterborne processions, followed by aquatic contests.

One unique custom on Ibiza used to be the lighting of nine fires outside homesteads on St John's Eve. These were used as targets for *feu de joie*. In fact firearms often played a sensational part in rural celebrations. Outside some of the old churches such as San Miguel, there is a stone platform known as *es mac de fer trons* (literally the thundermaking stone) upon and around which the young men of the village cavorted in an antique spiral dance known as *es caragol* (the snail), firing into the air at intervals. The Arab influence may once again be read into this preoccupation with firearms.

The local dialect of Ibizenc is based on the Catalan tongue, though often inflected in a different way, and corrupted by the use of some words which are purely Ibizan. But though this language, which sounds very strange to foreigners, is the first language of many Ibizans, they all understand and speak Spanish.

12 The Town of Ibiza

The Dalt Vila, the Ibizenc dialect name for the citadel high above the modern town, also dominates the harbour. Nothing could be more picturesque and, what is more, this unique group of ancient monuments and houses which are still lived in, tell the visitor much about the island's embattled history.

First of all this town perched on its precipice was Roman; later it was crowned by a Moorish Palace, the Almudaina. In medieval times and thereafter it became the site of the cathedral and the palace of the bishop, the Castle and an archaeological museum accommodated according to period in three distinct parts of what was originally the Town Hall or Ayuntamiento. These are all grouped together at the highest level, so that from every angle they are seen silhouetted against the sky, with the sea spread out below. Ibiza was granted the title of city by a Royal Charter dated 22 October 1783.

The Moorish defence system, which was strong enough to withstand Christian onslaught in the thirteenth century, has disappeared. This consisted of three lines of alternate walls and ditches against attack from the sea. But in the event the well co-ordinated crusading forces first landed 1500 infantry and some cavalry and set up camp, preparatory to bombarding the heights. It seemed as though a siege would follow, but in fact only the outer line of defence had to be breached, because by an act of treachery a secret passage had been left open on the landward side after its existence had been divulged to the invaders. The defenders were then utterly overwhelmed by the unexpected onrush of the enemy.

The present walls, which seem to tie the old city together, and are responsible for its beautiful silhouette, are predominantly sixteenth century. They were commissioned by Charles I of Spain, the Holy Roman Emperor, who is perhaps better known to us as Charles V or Charlemagne. At that time Spain was at the height of its power. The work was put into the hands of Juan Bautista Calvi, an Italian engineer, and took 30 years to complete. The cost of 50,000 ducats was a sum so large that nearly half had to be borrowed from the Archbishop of Valencia, who was never fully repaid, though it may be some consolation that he was eventually canonized. The two main gates, leading higher still, are comparatively near sea level. The Portal Nou, in a bastion not far from the west end of the Paseo Vara del Rey, the town's modern thoroughfare, leads by way of a tunnel towards a maze of cobbled passages and steep flights of steps set at all angles, so that the best principle for direction-finding is always to struggle uphill. But the gate on the side overlooking the quays, and above the town market, is the easier approach. The Puerta de las Tablas derives its name from an impressive entablature bearing the royal arms of Spain and a Latin inscription commemorating the achievements of King Philip II—the one who married our Tudor Queen Mary—and his Captain-General in incorporating Ibiza and, incidentally, the whole of the Iberian peninsula into his realm. The massive entrance, set deep into rising ground, looks out over a causeway which was once a drawbridge, and is flanked by niches containing two mutilated Roman statues, one of them of the goddess Juno. The mutilations may well have been the work of the Vandals, who made a practice of such behaviour.

Inside the gate one is confronted by an arcade which seems to grow out of the rock. This is where vendors have set up their stalls for the sale of all manner of things, but mostly souvenirs of authentic local workmanship. The easiest gradients to the summit can be reached by passing through an arch at the end of the first cobbled, arcaded street, to reach the Avenida Generalissimo Franco—otherwise known as Sa Carrossa, because it is fit for motor cars and does not peter out into blind alleys or at the foot of steps. People energetic enough to proceed under their own power, and who incidentally will see far more as they climb, should initially likewise bear left and follow the *avenida* past gardens and bougainvillaea-draped restaurants to arrive on the outer wall near the Santa Lucia bastion—where there is nothing below but a rough slope and eventually rocks and breaking waves which from this height look as though they are edged with lace. This is a good place for a short walk along the ramparts, where there are plane trees giving some shade, and also an intriguing view of the jumble of roofs of Sa Peña, the fishermen's quarter, at the turning point of land. There are six other bastions, all of them named after saints, and it is possible to walk almost without interruption along the sections of walls which link them. From Santa Lucia bastion onwards there are presented many opportunities for short cuts or diversions, away from the *avenida* which has had to swing back in order to negotiate the gradients. The visitor on foot who has chosen the steeper, more direct route will arrive soon at the domed church of San Domingo, which was the conventual church of the Dominicans. It has tiled domes, and a plain white-washed exterior, but inside is to be found a wealth—one might even say a riot—of baroque decoration. The Dominican monastery is nowadays occupied by the Ayuntamiento, a transfer of civic functions which has made it possible for the original town hall opposite the Cathedral to be turned into a museum. Near the Dominican church there is an enticing postern gate set in the next series of walls, but this is deceptive as far as the average sightseer is concerned, since it leads out on to a cliff walk—no railings or protective devices here—along a wild and undeveloped section of the headland. Our way should be to keep close to the walls, and by way of the Plaza España and Calle Santa Maria to find another, inward-facing gate called Sa Portello, after which, though the ascent remains steep, one is within sight of the goal.

The Plaza de la Catedral is dominated, almost impartially, by several fine buildings. The original Ayuntamiento uses its fine rooms to house archaeological collections and specimens gathered from all over the island. There are remains of the Almudaina beside the Cathedral, which has an irregular tower surmounted by a nobbly pyramid reminiscent of certain Punic mausolea, such as occur in Tunisia. The Cathedral is open to the public, but usually only in the morning. According to precedent it was built on the site of a mosque as soon as possible after the Reconquest, but came in for major rebuilding and restoration in the eighteenth century, so that the belfry is about all that remains of the original concept. The view from the parapet of the plaza, more than 91 metres above sea level, is the best of all, being nearly the highest, and completely unobstructed. The interior of the cathedral contains a great many beautiful items of church furniture and religious art, notably a very early retable behind the main altar, paintings and the Stations of the Cross in alcoves. Also there is an interesting memorial to the fallen in the Civil War of 1936, when the town was bombed. The body of the cathedral is lofty, painted white, but with details picked out in gold. Much of the church's treasure is on display in the episcopal museum, which is reached through a door south of the altar; stairs lead to collections of vestments and many other precious and venerated objects.

The return trip downhill must be the time for dallying

through narrow indeterminate alleys equipped with irregular steps and lined by secretive houses, built one above another and often sharing the same foundations. This also might be a time for visiting the studios owned usually by foreign artists who have made this place their own, and where all are welcome, whether or not they are likely to be buyers. There will also be indications as to the whereabouts of restaurants, bistros and cafés of different sorts and conditions, but none very large, because of the limitations imposed by the site upon the architecture. With any luck, too, one may stray into less ordered passageways inhabited by swarthy Ibizans, and memorable not only for characteristically local sights, sounds and smells, but for the occasional anonymous and derelict church. Hopefully even a haphazard descent will hit off the outer wall somewhere near the Plaza del Sol and the Portal Nou, through which the explorer can move towards a more familiar world. All in all, the Dalt Vila is a place of sheer enchantment, and fulfils all the expectations aroused by picture postcards and travel brochures.

But though the old part of the town is the showpiece, it by no means exhausts the pleasures of Ibiza town. The waterfront has the fascination of all such places, and is kept busy by coastal shipping and the regular steamship services operating from Valencia, Alicante and Majorca, as well, of course, as the island of Formentera, which is to be seen low on the horizon to the south. Fishing boats and the yachting marina are further along the bay, to the east of the main port. The quays are a pleasant mixture of functional warehouses, shipping offices, bars and restaurants with outside tables, confronting which there is an obelisk commemorating Ibiza's corsairs and their many engagements in their fast *zebecs,* the sailing vessels made of native pinewood. Most memorable of all these daring exploits seems to have been the taking in 1806 of the vastly bigger and better gunned British brig *Felicity,* after a glorious and bloody battle.

Every side street behind the quays can reveal some special fascination. In many of them, craftsmen may be seen at work in their small and often dark shops. Any of these is likely to be willing to undertake odd jobs while you wait, such as mending a sandal or a bag, or sewing on a button. Most people will find the market a magnetic attraction, not only for its shapes and sights and sounds and smells, but for the opportunities it gives of seeing the Ibizan citizens going about their everyday concerns amongst the produce of their island. By walking along the quay towards the mole at the west point of land, one skirts the fishermen's quarter of Sa Peña, a maze of cobbled streets and steps, huddled very close together, and disorderly in its random architecture. The impression is that here at least the inhabitants live their own lives, separate from tourism and in their natural and highly-coloured life style. It might be a good plan to take the path for a short distance beyond the mole before cutting back into the labyrinth on the return trip to the harbour and better-charted territory.

The life of the modern town is concentrated almost exclusively on either side of the Paseo Vara del Rey, the broad tree-lined avenue with a central island, which is the main thoroughfare running from near the port in the direction of the airport and towards the west of the island beyond San José. The ornate and lively monument at its centre commemorates the Ibizan general Vara del Rey, who distinguished himself in the Cuban War of Independence in 1810. The avenue named after him is not only the town's social centre, ideal for the evening *paseo* or ritual Spanish walkabout, but immensely popular with foreigners taking advantage of its pavement cafés. If you sit there long enough, much of the world will come your way, some smart, some hippies, some foreigners who have integrated well with the island of their choice, and of course many, many tourists. The end of the avenue nearest the harbour seems to be a gathering place for country people, many of them with a gipsy-like swarthiness, who seem to be awaiting impassively for something to happen—perhaps just *mañana*. But for a sight of the townswomen decked out in traditional finery the best place to go is Sunday Mass at the very small, plain, but originally fortified church of San Telmo, the patron saint of local seamen, and therefore not far from the quays and the Obelisk of the Corsairs.

Not only is the Paseo Vara del Rey a meeting place for all nations, but it is exceedingly useful to all comers, being also the town's principal business street, with all kinds of offices and some shops and, above all, banks and currency exchanges, taxi ranks and the Tourist Office which, incidentally, runs an efficient room-finding service. The old-established Montesol Hotel is at the seaward end of the avenue, on one corner, but the *hostals* or inns, about which one would be well advised to seek advice before booking in, are mostly to be found in the vicinity of the harbour, a part of the town which though lively and picturesque is not judged to be too healthy, since this town has been known to have trouble with its drainage system, such as it is. The Tourist Office will also advise on night life, which is ebullient and varied in the town itself, though more stereotyped in neighbouring resorts. The bull ring is to the north, between the sea and the Avenida Ignacio Wallis which leads north-west towards the centre of the island and San Antonio Abad. But the standard of sport here is low, so that it is not to be recommended to people expecting that the ceremonial and the expertise will compensate for any cruelty.

The Punic necropolis and the museum attached to it are to the left of the suitably named Via Punica, which runs parallel to the Avenida de España, which is virtually a narrower continuation of the Paseo Vara del Rey. The name Es Puig des Molins has been given to the hillside site because it once had a great many windmills; these are now gone. The correct name for the series of catacombs carved out of the rock, and which are said to contain more than 4000 graves, is the Necropolis of Ereso. A large proportion of their original contents—or at least a representative assortment of artefacts from different periods of Punic burial—are displayed in excellent order in the museum. The exhibits include sarcophagi, pottery, masks and figurines of Carthaginian deities, including many of the great goddess Tanit, domestic utensils, strange painted ostrich eggs—strange because the habitat of these birds is so very far from the Mediterranean—jewellery, and many other objects as interesting to the casual visitor as to the specialist.

The museum and a section of the necropolis are open to the public mornings and late afternoons, but those visitors who feel that the catacombs are too morbid, or just too claustrophobic, may study models in the museum.

13 The Rest of the Island

The Moors divided Ibiza into five administrative districts: Alhueth, Xarch, Benizamid, Portumany and Algarb. Beyond the inherent fascination of these outlandish names they are of little significance because the Christian conquistadors renamed them respectively Cuarton de Llan de la Villa (the metropolitan district), Santa Eulalia, Balanzat, Portmany and Las Salinas. The number was subsequently reduced to four, with two being held by Guillermo de Montgri, the Archbishop of Tarragona, in acknowledgement that his contributions in finance and manpower to the expedition had been more than double that of his partners.

Because of the way the land lies there is no continuous coast road. The nearest approximation to such a thing is the route from Ibiza to Es Cana, to the north-east of Santa Eulalia del Rio; otherwise every road splays out from the capital to the furthest corners of the island. Distances are short; for instance it is only 16 kilometres from Ibiza town to San Antonio Abad by a road which goes through the central small town of San Rafael, from where roads branch off to the north and east of the island.

San Antonio is the best known, and easily the most crowded of the island's resorts; in fact its growth has been so rapid and overwhelming that it is difficult to realise that not long ago it was a quiet fishing harbour. All the town has to show of its original identity is a fourteenth-century fortified church guarded by two towers. The rest is new, with the town's life scattered around its port and in the hotels which flank it to some distance from the small square which remains the town's centre, and where there are bars and discotheques and the usual entertainments for foreigners, not all of whom are English. This is a resort which particularly appeals to Germans in spite of the fact that except for a bare 182 metres stretch reached after a short walk, there is no proper beach. The thing to do is to take a boat to one of the many bays on either side. Because this is a real necessity, services are frequent. If possible a visit should be made to the underground and ruined church of Santa Inés, on the outskirts of the town and reached by the San José road. This is important enough to have been designated a National Monument. Another but more difficult land trip for which a guide should ideally be recruited, is to the Ses Fontanelles cave, near Cabo Nono, north of the resort. It has Bronze Age wall paintings, but not in very good condition.

The ferries to Port del Torrent and Cala Bassa, around the bay to the west, run at half-hour intervals, and there is also a bus service. Port del Torrent has a water-ski school, and both bays have ideal bathing and swimming conditions, also beach bars for drinks and light refreshments, so that there is no need to carry packed lunches. Cala Grasio, north of the town, is also very pleasant and easy to get to. More ambitious trips can be arranged to the two attractive northerly harbours of San Miguel and Portinatx, or to the islands off the west coast, particularly Isla Vedra. The attraction here is utter wildness, birds, and towering cliffs riddled with caves, all rising to 382 metres.

Though San Antonio Abad is a hive of activity during the summer months, winter spells an almost total shut-down, making it and its now spectre-like white hotels seem like a ghost town. Ibiza town reasserts itself as capital of the island during the off-season. Further exploration is easy in both cases, and in particular there are opportunities for making detours when travelling from one to the other in search of something out of the ordinary.

Figueretas, the suburb of hotels and apartment blocks which has been developed to compensate for Ibiza town's lack of beach, is only two kilometres from the town centre, or a short walk over the hump of the Puig des Molins. It has a regular bus service from the Ibiza town terminal, near the Hotel Montesol on the Paseo Vara del Rey. When the Playa de Ses Figueretas becomes crowded, there could be more room further on, at the Playa d'en Bossa, which is also well provided with hotels, bar/restaurants and entertainments. There is a more direct route west which bypasses these two resorts.

When starting out from Ibiza, the road to take is the Avenida de España, then to fork left towards the airport instead of continuing to San José. The airport road passes through the small village of San Jorge, where, to the right, there is a small fortified church with its cloisters, very typical of the fourteenth-century village churches which were designed to double up as a refuge for their communities whenever raids were signalled. Their crenellations and battlements upon which guns could be mounted have a very North African appearance, which is ironical since it was the Moors against whom they were armed. Some churches are even known to have had cannon emplacements on their roofs.

The even smaller church of San Francisco de Paula is at the northern corner of the saltpans, for which the road heads after passing the airport. This is the parish church for salt workers. It is unusual in having no burial ground attached, the reason being that the salinity of the soil would prevent decomposition—an unacceptable state of affairs here, though in other parts of the world it might be regarded as a virtue. The saltpans lie slightly below sea level, which means that sea water can be admitted, and sluices closed, leaving the sun to do the rest by evaporation, which has been calculated as 1200 litres per square metre in the course of a year. In all there are some 40 distinct saltbeds, producing in excess of 100,000 tones of salt annually, a large proportion of which goes by ship to northern Europe by way of the small port of La Canal, near the end of the road. Salt was a state monopoly until 1871, when it was sold to a private company for as little as 1,160,000 pesetas. According to season, the salt is piled into sparkling pyramids when awaiting shipment, which creates a transformation scene comparable to lunar photographs until one is brought back to earth by the sight of pines and dunes fringing an area which has been worked—though naturally with less mechanisation—for thousands of years.

Close to the end of the road there is a small beach called Playa sa Trincha. This is a dead end, and must be the turning point. If the idea is to explore the coast to the west it will be necessary to return to the fork in the road beyond the airport, and to turn left on to a straight stretch signposted to San José. Much of the land on either side is devoted to horticulture, kept productive by irrigation channels which are an inheritance from the period of Moorish domination. Sometimes vines are trained over the water, and serve the double purpose of keeping it cool while themselves deriving benefit. Five kilometres before reaching San José, on rising ground to the left, there is a small holy grotto, signposted as Cova Santa, which might be worth visiting, though it is nothing at all spectacular, but more an illustration of peasant simplicity and faith.

The mountains into which the road winds are mostly to the left. They are to scale with the rest of this not very large island, their highest peak reaching only 475 metres. The inland village of San José has a reputation for having preserved its folk lore with the greatest purity, and it makes almost compulsory halting places for excursions, even though there is no hotel. The eighteenth-century baroque church is the principal attraction, and has a great many beautiful features in the interior, such as an ornate altarpiece, a painted octagonal pulpit and many pictures. A road above the village leads to Cala Vadella, and off this there is an even twistier and narrower one to Cala d'Hort, an inlet of deep water from which there is an excellent view of Isla Vedra. This section of the coast is one of the most recent to attract development. Beyond San José, and left of the village of San Agustin and its church on a ridge, a detour will lead down to Cala Bossa and Port del Torrent—two of the best beaches easily reached from San Antonio Abad.

Because the north coast is rugged and roadless, anyone staying at San Antonio who wishes to explore the north and east parts of the island will first have to drive to inland San Rafael rather than risk the one alternative, which keeps inside the coastline on average about 2.5 kilometres, but which is not to be recommended. The safer route may be taken without regret, because San Rafael's church on a low hill manages to give a grandstand view of almost the whole island. Just to the south there is a country club and sports centre.

The direct route from Ibiza to the north misses out San Rafael but is joined by a linking cross-country road. Before that junction there is a fork, one prong of which heads for road's end at San Miguel, and the other for San Juan Bautista and Portinatx. The route to San Miguel goes through the village of Santa Gertrudis with the usual old fortified church with narrow slits for windows and a flat roof upon which armament could have been mounted. But the church of San Miguel, 16 kilometres from Ibiza, is reckoned as being the most perfect amongst its contemporaries. Since it was the church of the old bishopric its proportions are statelier, and its interior design not quite so simple as those of the true village churches. Again, and for the usual strategic reasons it is built on a hill, for which reason, in common with Santa Eulalia del Rio's church, it is known locally as the Puig de Missa. The forecourt to the church is paved with flagstones and surrounded by arcades—making an ideal gathering place for the villagers in times of danger or celebration, and in these days for communal gossip after the celebration of Mass. Port San Miguel is about four kilometres further north.

The second branch from the Ibiza road veers a little east of north after crossing the Rio de Santa Eulalia, which is something to be remarked upon, since it is the only permanent flow of water the island can boast; other watercourses, usually marked on the map as *torrente* are seasonal only, or carry floodwater after a rainstorm. This route leads through the fertile red soil of land which is under intense cultivation and produces all manner of cereal crops, fruit and vegetables. In particular, the fig trees are propped up into umbrella-like shapes, and not trained or allowed to grow freely, as elsewhere. The farmhouses or *fincas* are well settled into the landscape, despite their glaring whiteness. Indoors they are equally simple and austere, and consist traditionally of three sections; *sa casa de geure* (the house to sleep in), *sa casa des carro* (the cartshed) and *sa casa des gra*, or granary. They are whitewashed inside and out. Even the humblest roadside cottages go in for flowers outside their front doors and on window ledges. In driving around the country one can understand why so many foreigners have settled into small country properties.

Further along the road to San Juan Bautista there is a turning to the left to San Lorenzo, near which there is a most important site marked on the map as *Poblado Fortificado*. This explains it fully. Balafi is a fortified enclave of dwelling houses provided with two towers for defence. Entrance to these in times of emergency was provided by doors set high in their walls and provided with ladders which could be drawn up when everyone was safely inside. There is more than an echo here of the round towers of Ireland.

San Juan Bautista is a very short distance off the main road to the coast, on a turning which leads to the pretty harbour and resort of Cala San Vicente. This attractive, rather remote place is protected from the north by Punta Grossa, where there are interesting caves. These include Es Cuieram, a Punic temple dedicated to Tanit and excavated in 1907. But the adventurous should be warned: such places on Ibiza are not manned or equipped for safety as for instance the caves of Majorca which have been 'groomed', as it were, for the benefit of tourists.

San Juan rates as a small town, more than a village, in spite of having not very many houses. It claims to be the capital of the northern region. There is, vaguely, a mountain air about the place, though the altitude is only just over 200 metres. But everything on this small-scale island must be treated proportionately and with respect. As usual, the church is worth a visit, and in any event its terraces, which are really ramparts, make a restful stopping-place. The reredos is the most striking and valuable feature in the interior. In fact one may take this to be generally true of all these churches, whose history and style are apt to be uniform.

Returning to the main road, one follows it on its now serpentine progress down to the sea above Cala Charraca, where it runs along the edge of a cliff towards Portinatx, a place of beautiful beaches and clear water, a kind of civilised enclave carved out of the very wildest Ibizan coast. It may be that this lovely place suffers a little from the throes of rapid development, but these show signs of abating as it settles into the land- and seascape. Because the coast is rocky except in the coves, this makes a good centre for skin-diving, and most forms of water sports are catered for, including fishing. Suitable tackle is for sale or hire, and this seems to be a good place for purchasing sheepskin goods, probably because the hills behind are grazed by flocks of sheep, and they are likely to be locally made. The flocks are minded by women, often knitting, and dressed in a simplification of the older peasant costume. Shells are also a good buy here.

To be on the safe side, travellers by road wishing to explore the remainder of the coast between San Vicente and Ibiza town should not attempt what seems to be the obvious coastal route. However if the weather has been good, and after taking advice, it is possible to do just that by heading for San Carlos—once famous for lead mines—and eventually reaching Santa Eulalia after by-passing nearby Es Cana, which has grown into a popular resort. Otherwise it is better to return to the north-south road beyond San Juan Bautista, and continue to the crossroads just south of the Rio de Santa Eulalia.

In contrast to Es Cana, Santa Eulalia seems in the past to have turned its back upon the sea, though modern building projects have reversed the trend. Many of these are in the best of taste, keeping to traditional designs, resulting in tiers of white houses with arched patios fitting into the slopes above the sea. The neighbourhood is fertile, and grows garden crops in profusion, each rapidly succeeding another so as to make the fullest possible use of the land and available water. As it happens, the well-sung river is only 11 kilometres in length, and is sometimes in danger of drying up, but since it is unique it must be marvelled at as something of a natural phenomenon.

There is something unique too about the Puig de la Missa on the hill a little removed from the modern town. As usual, its church was built on the site of a mosque, though in this instance the Islamic entrance has been preserved in the form of horseshoe arches leading to precincts. And, most unusually, the Moorish buildings were in use for Christian worship well into the sixteenth century, that is until the time of its rebuilding, in 1568. Even at that date it was judged to require fortification and shelter for the local population in times of imminent danger, when they would be summoned from the fields by the church's great bell. The church of Nuestra Señora de Jesus contains what experts evaluate as Ibiza's most important ecclesiastical treasure: a beautiful carved and painted Gothic reredos designed and executed in Valencia. Other things to look for are the Stations of the Cross in tiles, and life-sized brightly painted statues, one of them of the Madonna robed in black velvet, and the effigy of the dead Christ laid out prostrate in a glass case, as though just taken from the Cross.

There are many incidentals to look for outside the church, besides the scatter of small white cubed houses with their flamboyent displays of flowers on the slopes. A walk makes the circuit of the church, leading past prickly pears upon which lovers have scratched their names. Mallow and fennel grow in profusion below a small cemetery, through the gate of which one can see the compartments in the inner walls in which the coffins are rested—on a leasehold basis. Many of them have little tributes arranged outside, reminiscent of the votive objects of Punic burial grounds. At one side of the church there is what is called the Barrau Museum, which is not a museum as such, but which contains a collection of the works of the Catalan Impressionist painter of that name.

The town of Santa Eulalia at sea level was popular with tourists many years before the holiday boom came to Spain and the Balearic Islands. It had, and has, a special atmosphere, though there is not much to it: really not much more than one main street, the Calle San Jaime, one shaded plaza, the Paseo Alameda, several side streets of small shops and a bus-stop in the Plaza de España on the landward side of the main street. There is a very wide choice of bars and cafés, also excellent restaurants, because this little town has enjoyed a long-standing reputation for good food. Most of the development has been restricted to the outskirts of the town, and especially away from the old village. The town's satellites, which include Playa d'es Cana to the north-east, and La Siesta and Cala Llonga further south, all have their quota not only of hotels, beaches, swimming pools and entertainments, but of apartments to rent, as for instance at Punta Arabi, where Spanish-style bungalows are part of a holiday complex, set among pine trees.

This is a beautiful coast, but not nearly as wild as the opposite northern one is, and there are excellent views from the road back to Ibiza town, which passes through the little town of Jesús, whose fourteenth-century parish church has—dare I say it?—a reredos which is considered to be almost the equal of Santa Eulalia's. Jesús stands at a fork of the road leading to Talamanca with its tall hotels strung out along the bay on the eastern side of Ibiza's harbour, and which like Cala de ses Figueretas on the opposite side, plays a supporting role for the antique town which has no space for a beach playground.

14 Formentera

In more senses than one Formentera maintains a low profile; low on the horizon as seen from Ibiza or from out to sea, its only important geographical features, the two lagoons. There are besides a great many sand dunes and farmhouses with usually no more than one storey, clinging to the land; altogether a spot without much excitement and therefore restful for the visitor who is content to spend most of his holiday on a beach. More detailed vital statistics show that this island beyond an island measures 115 square kilometres, and that its basic road system, which runs centrally three ways from the mini-capital, San Francisco de Javier, rather like the legs of the Isle of Man's emblem, eovers in all about 30 kilometres. The island's perimeter measures 59 kilometres and its highest point, La Mola in the east, reaches only 192 metres.

The narrow Freos strait separates Ibiza from Formentera beyond Punta de Portas, the headland south of Las Salinas saltpans. The 17 kilometre crossing takes 1½ hrs by steamer, but less by launch. A chain of sandy islands are skirted on the port side, with lighthouses and buoys to mark what would otherwise be a precarious channel. Espalmador is the biggest of these uninhabited islands and has the best beaches. Es Penjats, Pou, Espardell and Espardello are others, all north of Cala Sabina, the mother island's small port.

Even though Formentera's chasm is insidious, and creeps up upon one, this begins to happen immediately upon arrival, being heralded by palms and lagoons evocative of the South Seas. The Estang del Peix, or fishpond, was formerly used for the cultivation of fish and it is now popular for water ski-ing, and as a safe anchorage for small pleasure craft. The Estang Pudent to the east of the causeway and separating the two, has a name meaning—let's face it—'stinking', which does not immediately commend it. North of this shallower lagoon there are salt pans which are said to rival Ibiza's in output if not in size. This was one of the traditional exports of the island from early times onward. Wheat was the other, and it was shipped to Rome in sufficient quantities for the island to become known by a corruption of the Latin word *frumentaria,* meaning granary. The cultivation of cereal crops is still important, as is the raising of cattle, but tourism has taken some hold recently, rather belatedly, following the development of the resort of Es Pujols in 1972, with similar schemes following elsewhere.

Because the island is level except where there are hills towards the east and the south, one way to get about is by bicycle. These may be hired on arrival. Bus services also coincide with steamer times, and some cars and mopeds may be hired. A tarmac road runs the length of the island from La Sabina, through San Francisco Javier (with a branch to Playa d'es Pujols) and on past Es Calo—another possible place to stay—through the inland village of Nuestra Señora del Pilar with its dazzling white houses, to the La Mola lighthouse, above the cliffs of the east coast. The third leg of the road system runs more or less south, through countryside of stone-walled fields and white houses which have few outward looking windows, and very paintable windmills, as far as the watchtower called Il Torre d'es Cap, above Cabo Berberia.

The key to the history of Formentera lies in one negative characteristic: it proved, time and time again, to be indefensible, and therefore prey to repeated attack. In 1246, at the time of the reconquest of the islands, it was ceded by the Archbishop of Tarragona to the Frankish overlord Berenguer Renart on the understanding that he would resettle it, but such schemes were never successful for protracted periods. In the eighteenth century, when the fortified church of San Francisco Javier was built, the island was defended by a force of native militiamen—a Balearic Dad's Army— who showed great fortitude in manning their island against the Berber pirates who infested that part of the Mediterranean. The island had been repopulated from Ibiza—hence there is no difference in racial type, though it may be thought that the present inhabitants show an even greater simplicity and unworldliness. Following his visits in 1866 and 1888, the Hapsburg Archduke was particularly impressed by the islanders' longevity, and put it down to their leisured way of life, despite the necessity for survival.

The 'capital' of San Francisco Javier—named after the great missionary—is a microcosm of capitals elsewhere: it has a central square, banks, a post office, a telephone office, some cafés, bars and restaurants, and a doctor and a chemist housed on its outskirts. The fortified church, within the walls of which a proportion of the population could take refuge in case of need, was built in 1738, and contains some simple primitive murals. This and the coastal watchtowers are the only historic buildings to distract the attention from the beaches and their sparkling waters. The town of San Fernando, second most important of this central road, is straggling, and has enough amenities to satisfy the traveller along what has been not much more than a distance of one kilometre. From here a turning leads through pines and dunes to Es Pujols with its idyllic combination of white sand, miniature headlands and the clearest of water, with quieter beaches to be explored both to the east and west. The round watchtower of Punta Prima, which juts out to sea, is one of those which ringed all the Balearic islands against attack from the Arab raiders of North Africa.

The nine-kilometre drive (or bicycle ride) from San Fernando takes the explorer to Es Calo, another seaside village, one which possesses a natural harbour. The road keeps inland after Es Calo, and begins to twist and turn in its efforts to climb what for Formentera are prodigious heights. The sea remains within sight and sound as one goes through Nuestra Senora del Pilar, the last village before reaching the lighthouse on the east coast. This is a place of splendid cliff views, with caves to explore, but with few opportunities for swimming.

The Playa de Mitjorn on the south side of the island has been judged the best beach, because it is the longest. The frame is the typical pine-and-dune stage setting. All this extends for about eight kilometres to the far side of the smaller development at Arenals. One can guarantee that though this island, and this beach, have recently been 'discovered', there is plenty of room for all. Cala Sahona, on the west coast, is on a much smaller scale, and as such has its devotees, especially as there is a modicum of adventurousness involved in reaching it, down an unusually wide and almost deserted valley, to emerge at the beach below Cabo Punta Rosa.

Altogether Formentera is a paradise among islands, and though it is growing in an effort to please those people who seek it out, so far it has not lost its integrity, nor as a holiday haven has it become presumptuous by supplying anything in excess of the simpler pleasures.

Index